Grammar through Stories

···

Priscilla Karant

The American Language Institute, New York University

St. Martin's Press
New York

To Evelyn Langlieb Greer
for all the joy she has brought me

Editor: Naomi Silverman
Manager, publishing services: Emily Berleth
Project management: Denise Quirk
Art director: Sheree Goodman
Text design: Gene Crofts
Cover design: Herb Mills
Cover photo: Angel Franco/NYT Pictures

For information, write:
St. Martin's Press, Inc.
175 Fifth Avenue
New York, NY 10010

ISBN: 0-312-08361-0

Acknowledgments
    Josefowitz, Natasha. "Impressions from an Office." From *Path to Power: A Woman's Guide from First Job to Executive*, Addison-Wesley, 1980, 1990. Reprinted by permission of the author.
    Wall Street Journal. Chart. Reprinted by permission of the *Wall Street Journal*, © 1990 Dow Jones & Company, Inc. All Rights Reserved Worldwide.
    Daily News. "Got an idea? Send it to us." © New York Daily News, used with permission, and reproduced without alteration.
    Modell. "Not ŏ, dummy, ōō." Drawing by Modell, © 1978 The New Yorker Magazine, Inc.
    Price, Geo. "Mind if I smoke?" Drawing by Geo. Price, © 1978 The New Yorker Magazine, Inc.
    Save Our Cumberland Mountains. Photograph and logo. Used with permission of Save Our Cumberland Mountains.
    Orr, Beverly A. Photograph of "Ralph Nader." Used with permission of Beverly A. Orr.
    Levine, Melinda. Line drawing "Finders Keepers." Used with permission of Melinda Levine.
    Ramos, Arnaldo. Photograph of "Ben and Jerry eating ice cream." Used with permission of Arnaldo Ramos.

PREFACE

Grammar through Stories is a textbook for intermediate to advanced students who need to improve grammatical accuracy and fluency in English. To reach these goals, *Grammar through Stories* provides students with stories to listen to for specific grammar points. The text focuses on having students listen to stories, retell them, and react to them. The text comes with an audiocassette that allows students to work on their own.

Grammar through Stories challenges students with humorous and thought-provoking stories so that they can enjoy becoming more fluent in English. It is not meant to be a comprehensive grammar book, but rather a review of difficult structures that students who have studied grammar still struggle with.

▶ Why Use Stories?

Working with stories helps students develop a more accurate fluency because grammatical structures are more easily retained when grammar is used in context. Intermediate and advanced students are often proficient at filling in the blanks of grammar-book exercises without being able to produce accurate sentences in free writing or in conversation. There is frustration.

Language does not become one's own until it is used in real situations. In the classroom, instructors try to figure out how to make a rule "stick." While students may have problems remembering unrelated sentences, they tend to remember stories.

Grammar through Stories is a flexible text; you need not work in sequence. The organization of the book allows for selection of those exercises most appropriate for the needs of particular groups of students. No matter how you use this text, students enjoy the following benefits:

▼ Stories allow students to *review structures again and again* without feeling bored. Since students are focused on the story and not just on the mechanics of a sentence, their attention is greater.

▼ Students learn to *listen for grammar as well as content;* thus, they become more attuned to correct grammar when they use English.

▼ Students learn about some aspects of *U.S. culture* through these stories.

▼ *Real stories* capture the student's interest more than mere grammar exercises. Stories easily lead to other activities.

▼ Students become *active learners* in creating their own stories.

▼ Students *learn to question, to analyze, and to express their opinions.* In doing so, they develop their language skills.

▼Suggestions for Using This Book

Grammar through Stories contains thirteen chapters and is accompanied by a thirty-seven-minute cassette that contains the stories and the dictations for each chapter. In each chapter, there are ten focuses and a grammar review section. Instructors and students can choose which focuses they want to work on; they need not do every exercise in each chapter. They should choose focuses according to these criteria: the level of the class, the needs of the students, and the amount of class time. Each chapter has a photograph, chart, or cartoon to aid students in developing fluency.

The sections below include information on the following points:

▼ time recommended to allot for each focus
▼ hints for using the material with different class levels
▼ tasks recommended for homework
▼ suggestions for grouping students
▼ suggestions for working with groups
▼ suggestions for correcting students

Focus 1

A. Understand the Story (ten to twenty minutes)   Students listen to the story to identify the main idea. Then, in pairs, students write two or three sentences concisely summarizing the main points of the story. Students can present their sentences orally or write them on the blackboard. Instructors should have the class choose which sentences best summarize the story. While instructors should make corrections when needed, this exercise emphasizes comprehension and fluency.

Note: Instructors can play the tape or read aloud the transcript in Appendix 2.

B. Understand the Vocabulary (ten minutes)   In groups of two or three, students listen to the story again to try to figure out what specific words and expressions mean in the context of the story. The instructor should encourage students to guess by helping them with clues whenever necessary. Students who successfully figure out a meaning of a word should explain what helped them. The emphasis in this exercise is to make students better listeners.

For a more advanced class where the vocabulary items pose no difficulty, this exercise can be skipped. For a less advanced class, instructors can stop the tape after each sentence that contains the new word or expression.

Note: Instead of replaying the tape or rereading the whole story, the instructor can simply read aloud the sentences where the vocabulary appears.

Focus 2: Understand the Grammar (fifteen to twenty-five minutes)

A. Practice   While each story has students review many grammar points at once, this exercise highlights one or two areas. The instructor helps students review the highlighted grammar point, then students listen to the story again. This time they focus on a grammatical structure.

For a less advanced class, instructors need to go over with the students the Grammar Review at the end of each chapter before doing this exercise.

B. Edit   This exercise uses sentences from the story that pinpoint the errors students often make with the highlighted grammar point. Students should be encouraged to find the errors and make the necessary corrections on their own. They should be encouraged to explain their corrections. The emphasis here is accuracy.

C. Listen   Students listen to the story for a second time (or third time depending on level). Students should be encouraged to be more active listeners by having them list certain grammatical structures that are being pointed out in the story. Students are not expected to list everything but simply as many as they hear. The emphasis in this exercise is to help students pay more attention to grammatical structures when they are listening.

Focus 3: Retell the Story (fifteen to twenty-five minutes)

The first time the complete story is reconstructed, it can be done as a class. The instructor serves as a leader, stopping a student when he or she makes an error and choosing a student to correct the error and continue the story. Depending on the fluency of a class, the instructor can choose to correct the highlighted grammar, and/or other structure problems, and/or wrong facts, and/or pronunciation. While the emphasis is on accuracy, instructors should refrain from correcting every error with lower-level students. When the students have finished retelling the story, the instructor can pair the students for a second retelling of the story. This time each student tells the whole story while his or her partner listens and helps. The instructor should circulate to help students correct themselves.

For a more advanced class, the story can be retold once either as a class or in pairs. The instructor should vary the method used for different chapters. For a less advanced class, correction should be limited to biggest errors as not to overwhelm students with corrections.

Focus 4: Write the Story (ten minutes)

Students write a summary of the story in their own words. Students are not expected to remember all the details of a story but should be able to write a concise summary of it. Students should be encouraged to review their writing to check for the highlighted grammar point. This encourages accuracy. Giving students a time limit to write their summaries helps students develop fluency.

While students are writing, the instructor circulates to point out errors related to the highlighted grammar point. The instructor should encourage students to figure out the corrections to their grammar errors on their own when possible. Papers should be collected and corrected.

Students should hand in rewrites of their summaries, incorporating the suggested corrections. Students must be told to write titles, indent for paragraphs, and write legibly.

Focus 5: Discuss the Story (twenty to thirty minutes)

Before looking at the discussion questions, students should be encouraged to form their own questions based on the story. By having students think of the words *compare, contrast, react,* and *suggest,* the instructor can guide students to ask their own questions. Is there a controversy? If so, a question could be "Do you agree or disagree with . . . ?" If someone took an action, a question could be "If you had been the . . . , what would you have done?" The story could pose a need for a solution. If so, a question could be "What do you suggest . . . ?" For the first chapter, this exercise in formulating questions could be done in groups, in pairs, or with the whole class. After students present their questions, they can look at the exercise to see if they left out any questions they would like to discuss. During this exercise, the instructor should circulate to help students when necessary. The instructor should act as a moderator and a stimulator but should refrain from doing too much talking.

Whereas the emphasis here is fluency, instructors should encourage accuracy for the highlighted grammar points.

Note: If class time is limited, students can skip forming their own questions. Also, the instructor can direct students to choose just one question for their group to dicuss.

Focus 6: One-Minute Speech (ten minutes)

The instructor chooses two students to make a one-minute speech on any of the discussion questions. The one-minute time limit must be strictly enforced. Students should be encouraged to outline their ideas on an index card and to practice the speech at home. They are not to read while speaking. While a student is presenting a speech, the other students should jot down any errors they hear. The instructor should review these errors only after the student has finished speaking. Students can hand in texts of their speeches.

For a more advanced class, students can be challenged to give spontaneous one-minute speeches. For a less advanced class, the teacher should refrain from overwhelming the student with too many corrections.

Focus 7: Write Your Opinions (Homework)

Students choose a discussion question to write on. They should organize their ideas and support their opinions with specific examples. Before handing in their essays, students should be encouraged to proofread especially for grammar points discussed. Instructors should have students write three-part essays (introduction, main thesis, and examples and conclusion) and encourage them to do rewrites of their essays.

In a more advanced class, students can practice proofreading a classmate's paper. In a less advanced class, students can underline the highlighted grammar point that they incorporate in their writing. For example, if the chapter focuses on articles, students should underline all the nouns they use in their essay. This builds awareness.

Focus 8: Grammar Review (Homework)

Students take a grammar review test based on the original story. The grammar related to the highlighted grammar point of the chapter is in **bold**. Students should concentrate most on this grammar.

After testing themselves, students can refer to the transcripts of the stories in Appendix 2 for the correct answers. Students can also refer to Appendix 1 for explanations of words that confuse. Students should prepare questions on any answers they do not understand. Students should be prepared to explain their choices. For example, "I chose *dollar* not *dollars* because I need an adjective here. Adjectives do not take *s.*"

The instructor should *briefly* explain grammar points not focused on. Also, with a less advanced class, instructors can have students focus on highlighted structures only.

Focus 9: Dictation (Homework)

Students take a dictation from the tape at home. The dictation can be the whole story or a part of the story, depending on the needs of the student. Students can check their dictations themselves by referring to the transcripts in Appendix 2.

Focus 10: Storytelling (twenty to thirty minutes)

From a newspaper article, photograph, or personal experience, several students (one per group of three or four students) prepare a story to tell, incorporating the highlighted grammar point of the lesson. They prepare the story at home and tell it in small groups. The story should be limited to two minutes. It should be told, not read. Any new vocabulary items should be introduced before students present their stories. Group members can practice retelling the story to other groups while the storyteller helps out. Students should rotate as storytellers.

Note: Instructors can have students write out their stories for more composition practice. Students should be encouraged to do rewrites of any corrected writing.

Grammar Review

This section at the end of each chapter gives a more detailed analysis of the highlighted grammar points. Explanations are concise so that students can review the grammar on their own. This section can be referred to before, during, and/or after the exercises, depending on the students' needs.

Appendix 1

This section contains frequently confused words or expressions from the thirteen stories. Students can refer to this list whenever they come across these words in a story. At the end of this section, students can test themselves. Test answers are included at the end of the appendix.

Appendix 2

This section contains the transcripts of the taped stories. Students can refer to the transcripts when correcting their answers to Focus 8: Grammar Review and to Focus 9: Dictation.

Visuals

Each chapter has a photograph, cartoon, chart, or advertisement. Questions related to these visuals encourage critical thinking.

Reading

Instructors should encourage students to read newspapers in English during the semester. Besides reading for meaning, students should learn to examine the grammatical structures of sentences.

▼ Acknowledgments

I would like to thank Arnaldo and Emile Ramos, my husband and son, for all their love and support during this project while I tried out my stories on them. I also want to thank Sue and Joshua Karant, my sister and nephew, for their ideas and encouragement on this book. I want to give endless thanks to my mother who was always available to edit whatever I wrote. I want to thank my father, who was so proud of me that he made me feel I could accomplish what I wanted to accomplish. Tremendous thanks go to Lynne Hale, Panta da Silva, and Morgan Paolo da Silva Hale for taking care of me when my computer broke down. Lynne Hale was especially helpful in giving me suggestions after trying out my material with her classes. I want to thank Melinda Levine for always being quick to the rescue.

I also want to dedicate my book to those teachers at the American Language Institute—Miriam Dancy, Fred Malkemes, and Frank Ransom—who inspired me.

I want to thank all those instructors who field-tested my book and whose enthusiasm pushed me on. During the development of this book, the following reviewers provided helpful suggestions: Joan Gregg, New York City Technical College (CUNY); Dennis Hall, New Hampshire College, American Language and Culture Center; Jonathan Seely, University of Arizona; and Diane Yokel, University of Denver, English Language Center. Special thanks to Naomi Silverman, my editor, for all her ideas and support.

And of course, I want to thank those hundreds of students from New York University, Baruch College, and Borough of Manhattan Community College, whose joy at learning through stories motivated me to write this book.

CONTENTS

• •

12 *The New Illiteracy*   *131*

Give Americans a map and find out about the new illiteracy

Grammar Review: *If* Clauses   139

13 *Ben and Jerry*   *141*

Their mission to make money to give it away

Grammar Review: Inverted Word Order   149

TO THE STUDENT

• •

Have you studied English before but still feel frustrated by the grammar mistakes you make in your writing and in your speech? *Grammar through Stories* will help you pinpoint your problems in grammar while helping you improve your listening, speaking, writing, and critical thinking skills.

Each chapter has ten focuses to reach these goals. The accompanying audiocassette of the stories will allow you to review your troublespots as often as you need. The stories will teach you more about Americans and U.S. culture. The Grammar Review sections at the end of each chapter will provide helpful explanations of the grammar points highlighted in each story. Appendix 1 lists frequently confused words and phrases used in the stories. Appendix 2 contains the transcripts of the stories so that you correct your dictation and grammar on your own.

Grammar through Stories will help you if

▼ you plan to study in an English-speaking country
▼ you plan to work in an English-speaking country
▼ you plan to write in English
▼ you plan to take the TOFEL
▼ you need to increase your listening skills

Whether studying English is a hobby or a necessity, *Grammar through Stories* will make studying enjoyable and thought-provoking.

The Taxi Cab

Past Tenses
Reported Speech

FOCUS 1

A. Meaning Listen to the story on the tape. What is the main idea? With a partner, write two or three sentences that best summarize the main idea.

B. Vocabulary Do you understand the italicized words below? If not, listen to the story on the tape again. Try to understand what the following words mean after hearing them in the story. Can you guess the correct meaning? What words or sentences help you guess? Explain to a partner or your group members what you think these words mean.

hail	*swerve*	*meter*
accelerator	*raining cats and dogs*	*backseat driver*

FOCUS 2: Past Tense and Reported Speech

A. Past Tense The story you have just heard is told in the past tense. Some of these verbs are irregular. Underline the irregular verbs below.

decide	*come*	*see*
drive	*pass*	*steal*
want	*try*	*run*
tell	*jump*	*have to*

Do you know how to pronounce the past tense of regular verbs? With your partner, identify which of the above verbs have an "id" sound, a "t" sound, and a "d" sound. Practice saying all the verbs aloud. Check the Grammar Review in this chapter if needed.

B. Reported Speech When telling a story, most people use reported speech instead of direct quotations. Study the examples below carefully. Note how changes are made in *word order*, *verb tense*, *pronouns*, and *punctuation*. With a partner, practice changing these sentences to reported speech.

Examples

   a. Sue asked, "Where can I catch a cab?"
     Sue asked where **she could** catch a cab.

   b. Sue said to the driver, "Slow down!"
     Sue **told the driver to** slow down.

   c. Sue asked, "Is it far?"
     Sue asked **if it was** far.

1. Philip asked, "How much is it?"

2. Mary Ann said to the driver, "Take me to the train station."

3. Joshua said, "The bus will stop by the school."

4. Jessica asked us, "Have you been waiting long?"

C. Edit   Read the sentences below. Look for errors in past tense and in reported speech. Make the necessary corrections.

1. One of the women leaned forward and ask the driver how much do they owe him?

2. Neither knew how much did it cost?

3. When the cab stoped, the women jumpt in.

D. Listen   Now listen to the story again. Try to list as many past-tense verbs as you hear.

▶ FOCUS 3: Retell the Story

In pairs or as a class, retell the story you have just heard. Your instructor will stop you when you make a mistake. The next student corrects and continues the story.

▶ FOCUS 4: Write the Story

Write a summary of the story in your own words. Be sure to check the past tense forms, especially when using irregular verbs.

Facts on New York Taxi Drivers*
1. Ninety percent of all drivers are immigrants whose native language is not English.
2. Less than 1 percent of all drivers are women.
3. The average salary ranges from $21,000 to $30,000 a year.

*Source: *New York Times* 6 Oct. 1991, sect. 4, p. 7.

1. What are some reasons to explain the numbers of immigrants and the number of women driving cabs?

2. How do you think these facts compare with drivers in your country?

▶ FOCUS 5: Discuss the Story

Discuss the following questions with group members.

1. Describe how taxis are used in your country. How do they differ from taxis in the United States? (cleanliness, tipping system, male/female drivers, driving style, meter system, automatic doors)

2. Were you ever in a car when someone drove recklessly? If so, what did you say to the driver? *Use reported speech.*

3. Have you ever been in a car with a "backseat driver"? What did he or she say? How did that make you feel? What did you say in response to a backseat driver's comments? What term do you use for a backseat driver in your country?

4. Have you ever heard of someone's car or bicycle being stolen? Tell the story. *Use past tense.*

▼ FOCUS 6: One-Minute Speech
····································

> ▼ Choose one of the discussion questions above for your speech.
> ▼ Outline the points to be made.
> ▼ Time yourself at home while practicing the speech.

▼ FOCUS 7: Write Your Opinions
····································

> ▼ Write your opinions on any one of the discussion questions.
> ▼ Organize your ideas before writing.
> ▼ Support your opinions with specific examples.

▼ FOCUS 8: Grammar Review
····································

Read the following story. Circle the correct answers. Be prepared to explain your choices.

One (rainy, raining) day two women (**have decided, had decided, decided**) they wanted to (go to shopping, go shopping) at Bloomingdale's. They lived on the Upper West Side of Manhattan and were waiting (0, for) a bus to (**take, took**) them across (the, 0) Central Park to the store. That day (it, 0) was raining cats and dogs. The women knew it (**will, would**) be hard to get around the city on (so, such, such a) lousy day. So, when no bus (**comes, came, has come**) after a twenty-(minute, minutes) wait, the women (**have decided, had decided, decided**) to try to hail a cab. They (**try, tried, tryed**), but all the cabs (was, were) full. Finally, they (**have seen, had seen, saw**) (a, an) empty one. They both (**run, ran, have run**) out to the street and waved (furious, furiously) to make the cab (to stop, stopped, stop, stopping). But the empty cab (**passed, past, pass**) them by. They wondered why (**hadn't the cab, the cab hadn't**) stopped for them. Luckily, the light turned (to, 0) red and the cab (**have, had, had**) to stop. The women (**run, have run, ran**) to the cab, opened the door, and (**jumpt, jump, jumped**) in. The driver turned (around, over, in) and looked (surprising, surprise, surprised). The women didn't (**understand, understood**) why. Ignoring his (surprising, surprise, surprised) look, they (said, told) him to (**take, took**) them to Bloomingdale's.

Off he (**goes, went**). He (**has driven, drove, drives**) like a madman across (the, 0) Central Park with his (foot, feet) all the way down on the accelerator. Not only (he was, was he) swerving in and out of lanes, but he never even (**bothers, bothered, had bothered**) to stop (at, on, in) the stop signs. One woman told her friend how scared (**I am, she is, I was, she was**), but she didn't (**want, wanted**) to be a backseat driver. The other bravely (**shouts, shouted, has shouted**), "Would you mind (to slow, slowing) down?" She also told him that (**you are, you were, he was, he is**) driving (too, very) dangerously. The driver told the women (**don't, to not, not to**) worry as he continued to race to the store. Also, he (**has never put, never put, had never put**) the meter on. The women didn't understand what (**is was**) going on.

At last, they arrived (at, to, in) Bloomingdale's. Both women (**feel, felt, fell**) exhausted. Neither (**knows, knew, has known**) how much (**did the trip cost, does the trip cost, the trip costed, the trip cost**). So, one of the (womens, woman, women) leaned forward and (**ask, asked**) (to, 0) the driver how much (**do they owe, did they owe,**

they owed) him. The driver calmly (said, told), "Nothing, (ladys, ladies). I just (**stole, steal, had stolen**) the cab."

FOCUS 9: Dictation

From the tape, take a dictation. Check your writing by looking at the transcript in Appendix 2.

FOCUS 10: Storytelling

Now it is your turn to tell members of your group a story in the past tense.

- From a newspaper article, a photograph, or a personal experience, find a story you want to tell.
- Introduce new vocabulary to your group.
- Limit yourself to two minutes.
- Tell the story without reading or memorizing it.
- Have your classmates retell the story in pairs.

Extra Practice

Using reported speech, retell the following story to your neighbor.

Examples

a. "Are you late?"
You say: "He asked me if I was late."

b. "I'm leaving for work."
You say: "He told me he was leaving for work."

I'm leaving work late. I have to catch a 7:00 airplane at the airport. I feel nervous because I don't have much time. I go out to the street to try to hail a cab, but the taxis are all full. Finally, I see someone getting out of one, so I run like crazy to catch it. The driver is polite. He opens up the trunk and I throw in my luggage, get in the cab, and shut the door. The driver takes off. But it takes more than an hour to get to the airport because there was an accident on the highway. Anyway, we get to the airport. I have fifteen minutes to spare, so I rush out to grab my luggage. Meanwhile, the driver looks confused. He's searching through his pockets for the trunk key. He screams, "What did I to! I lost the key!" I'm feeling frantic. I scream, "What am I going to do? I can't leave without my baggage." A group of taxi drivers gather around to help us. I'm practically crying and so is the driver. One of the other drivers has an ax. They all decide to tear out the back seat to get my luggage. They succeed! I grab my luggage, give the driver a big tip, and thank all his helpers profusely. I run into the airport and make the plane.

GRAMMAR REVIEW
· · · · · · · · · · · · · · · · · · ·
Past Tenses
Reported Speech

▶ The Simple Past Tense

1. The **simple past tense** is used for a *completed action* in the past. It can be used with words like *yesterday, ago, last week*.

   I went to the library yesterday.

2. The simple past tense is used to show a *habitual past action*. It can be used with adverbs of frequency like *usually, often, never*.

   She never told me about the party.

3. To form the simple past tense of regular verbs, add *-ed*. See page 11 for spelling changes of regular verbs.

   We protest**ed** against the war.

4. To form the simple past of irregular verbs, memorize the list on pages 12–14.

5. To form a question or a negative statement in the simple past, add the auxiliary *did* and use the **base form** of the verb (without *-ed*).

   Did you **protest** against the war?
   I **did not protest** against the war.

▸ Other Ways of Expressing the Past

1. The words *used to* and *would* can also be used to show a *repeated action in the past*.

    I used to play tennis as a child.

    I would play tennis when the sun was out.

2. The **past continuous** stresses *duration* more than the simple past tense does. It describes a temporary activity that is in progress. Note the difference between the two.

    While I was waiting for a bus, it began to rain.

3. The **present perfect** shows a *connection to the present*.

    He has not called today.

    This statement shows that the speaker feels there is a possibility that he will still call. It means up to now he has done it.

    He did not call today.

    This statement shows that the speaker feels there is no more possibility that he will call today.

4. The **past perfect** shows a *completed action* that takes place *before another past action*.

    Before I came to New York, I had studied English.

    This statement shows that I first studied English and then I came. English speakers in the United States, however, often use the simple past for both actions. You can also say:

    Before I came to New York, I studied English.

▸ Pronunciation Rules for Simple Past Verbs

"D"

▸ Verbs that end with vowel sounds

I played with him.

▸ Verbs that end with *b, g, j, l, m, n, r, v, z*

   She called him up.

"ID"

▸ Verbs that end with a "d" or "t" sound

   I wanted to go.

"T"

▸ Verbs that end with *c, ch, f, gh, k, p, s, sh, x*

   He jumped in.

▸ Spelling Rules for the Simple Past Tense

1. When the next to last letter is a single vowel, double the consonant. (Exception: When the accent is on the first syllable, the consonant is not doubled, like in the word traveled.)

   stopped

   grabbed

2. When the verb ends with a consonant and a *y*, change the *y* to *i*.

   tried

   worried

3. When the verb ends in an *e*, add *d*.

   liked

   died

▸ Irregular Verbs in English

Here is an alphabetical list of most of the irregular verbs in English.

Base Form	Past	Past Participle
be (am, is, are)	was, were	been
bear	bore	born
beat	beat	beat
become	became	become
begin	began	begun
bend	bent	bent
bet	bet	bet
bite	bit	bitten
bleed	bled	bled
blow	blew	blown
break	broke	broken
bring	brought	brought
build	built	built
burst	burst	burst
buy	bought	bought
catch	caught	caught
choose	chose	chosen
come	came	come
cost	cost	cost
cut	cut	cut
dealt	dealt	dealt
do	did	done
dig	dug	dug
draw	drew	drawn
drink	drank	drunk
drive	drove	driven
eat	ate	eaten
fall	fell	fallen
feed	fed	fed
feel	felt	felt
fight	fought	fought
find	found	found
fit	fit	fit
fly	flew	flown
forbid	forbade	forbidden
forget	forgot	forgotten
forgive	forgave	forgiven
freeze	froze	frozen
get	got	got (or) gotten

Base Form	Past	Past Participle
give	gave	given
go	went	gone
grow	grew	grown
hang	hung	hung
have	had	had
hear	heard	heard
hide	hid	hidden
hit	hit	hit
hold	held	held
hurt	hurt	hurt
keep	kept	kept
kneel	knelt	knelt
know	knew	known
lay	laid	laid
lead	led	led
leave	left	left
lend	lent	lent
let	let	let
light	lit	lit
lose	lost	lost
lie	lay	lain
make	made	made
mean	meant	meant
meet	met	met
pay	paid	paid
put	put	put
quit	quit	quit
read	read	read
ride	rode	ridden
ring	rang	rung
rise	rose	risen
run	ran	run
say	said	said
see	saw	seen
sell	sold	sold
send	sent	sent
set	set	set
shake	shook	shaken
shine	shone	shone

Base Form	Past	Past Participle
shoot	shot	shot
shut	shut	shut
sing	sang	sung
sit	sat	sat
sleep	slept	slept
speak	spoke	spoken
speed	sped	sped
spend	spent	spent
split	split	split
spread	spread	spread
stand	stood	stood
steal	stole	stolen
stick	stuck	stuck
sting	stung	stung
strike	struck	struck
swear	swore	sworn
sweep	swept	swept
swim	swam	swum
swing	swung	swung
take	took	taken
teach	taught	taught
tear	tore	torn
tell	told	told
think	thought	thought
throw	threw	thrown
understand	understood	understood
wake	woke	waken
wear	wore	worn
win	won	won
wind	wound	wound
write	wrote	written

▼ Reported Speech

When **reporting a conversation,** English speakers usually use indirect speech, not direct quotations. Here are suggestions on how to make this change.

1. Change the punctuation.

   He said, "I want to apply to the university."

   He said **that** he wanted to apply to the university. (Add the word *that* in reported statements.)

   She asked, "Where have you been?"

   She asked where I had been.

2. Change the verb tense to agree with the verb in the introductory clause.

   He **said,** "They **will be** there."

   He **said** that they **would be** there.

3. Change the pronouns to agree with the introductory pronoun.

   They said, "**We** want **you** to succeed."

   They told **me** that **they** wanted **me** to succeed.

4. Change adverbs of time and place so that they logically agree with the change in tenses. Here are some common changes.

now	then
this	that
these	those
yesterday	the previous day
yet	by that time
today	that day
tomorrow	the next day

   I asked him, "Will I see you **tomorrow?**"

   I asked him if I would see him **the next day.**

5. Add *to* for positive commands and *not to* for negative commands.

   She said to me, "Come **on Monday and don't be late.**"

   She told me **to come** on Monday and **not to be** late.

6. When reporting a question that does not have a question word (like *who, where, what, how*), use *if* or *whether* to connect the question to the introductory clause.

She asked him, "Are you hungry?"

She asked him **if** he **was** hungry.

7. When reporting a question, change the word order. The subject comes before the verb.

He asked me, "Why do you think so?"

He asked me why **I thought** so.

Note: Noun clauses that come after *I know, I wonder, I'm not sure,* and *I didn't understand* follow the same word order as a reported-speech question.

"What does this mean?"

I know what this means.

I knew what this meant.

2

Women in the United States

Present Tenses

Impressions from an Office*
By Natasha Josefowitz

The family picture is on HIS desk.
Ah, a solid, responsible family man.
The family picture is on HER desk.
Umm, her family will come before her career.
HIS desk is cluttered.
He's obviously a hard worker and a busy man.
HER desk is cluttered.
She's obviously a disorganized scatterbrain.
HE is talking with his co-workers.
She must be gossiping.
HE's not at his desk.
He must be at a meeting.
SHE's not at her desk.
She must be in the ladies' room.
HE's not in the office.
He's meeting customers.
SHE's not in the office.
She must be out shopping.
HE's having lunch with the boss.
He's on his way up.
SHE's having lunch with the boss.
They must be having an affair.
The boss criticized HIM.

He'll improve his performance.
The boss criticized HER.
She'll be very upset.
HE got an unfair deal.
Did he get angry?
She got an unfair deal.
Did she cry?
HE's getting married.
He'll get more settled.
SHE's getting married.
She'll get pregnant and leave.
HE's having a baby.
He'll need a raise.
SHE's having a baby.
She'll cost the company money in maternity benefits.
HE's going on a business trip.
It's good for his career.
SHE's going on a business trip.
What does her husband say?
HE's leaving for a better job.
He knows how to recognize a good opportunity.
SHE's leaving for a better job.
Women are not dependable.

1. Which of these impressions seem true? Which seem untrue? Give examples to show why.

2. If these impressions were written about a man or a woman from your country, how would you change them?

*From *Path to Power: A Woman's Guide from First Job to Executive*, by Natasha Josefowitz, published by Addison-Wesley, 1980. Copyright 1990 by Natasha Josefowitz. Used by permission.

▟ FOCUS 1

A. **Meaning**   Listen to the story on the tape. What is the main idea? With a partner, write two or three sentences that best summarize the main idea.

B. **Vocabulary**   Do you understand the italicized words below? If not, listen to the story on the tape. Try to understand what the following words mean after hearing them in the story. Can you guess the correct meaning? What words or sentences help you guess? Explain to a partner or your group members what you think these words mean.

strides	*so-called*	*predominantly*
B.A.	*lawsuits*	*affordable*
gender gap	*shrinking*	

▟ FOCUS 2: Present Tenses

A. **Present Tenses**   The story you have just heard uses three different tenses—the simple present, the present continuous, and the present perfect—to indicate the present. Read the three sentences below. Can you explain how these tenses differ?

1. She **works every day.**

2. She **is working right now.**

3. She **has worked since** she was sixteen.

Now form your own sentences with the verbs below using the expressions *every day, right now,* and *since.*

smoke	*read*
play piano	*make her bed*

B. **Edit**   Read the sentences below. Look for errors in the verb tenses. Make the necessary corrections.

1. Since the 1960s, women are making tremendous strides in the United States.

2. Yet, despite these gains, a double standard is still existing.

3. When a child gets sick, the mother is the one who has stayed home.

C. **Listen**   Now listen to the story again. List as many verb tenses as you can hear.

▼ FOCUS 3: Retell the Story

In pairs or as a class retell the story you have just heard. Your instructor will stop you when you make a mistake. The next student corrects and continues the story.

▼ FOCUS 4: Write the Story

Write a summary of the story in your own words. Be sure to check the

Facts on Working Mothers in the United States*
1. Nearly 60 percent of all women have a job or are looking for one.
2. Twenty-three percent of women in the workplace have a child under three.
3. Half of those mothers who work are widowed, divorced, or separated.
4. Forty percent of those mothers who work have never married.

*Source: Bureau of Labor Statistics, 1991.

1. How do these figures compare to working women in your country? If there is a difference, please explain why.

2. What facilities are available for children of working women in your country? Describe the situation.

FOCUS 5: Discuss the Story

Discuss the following question with group members.

1. Have you experienced a double standard in your life? If so, give specific examples from your home life or your work experience.
2. Do you know of a woman who balances her role as wife, mother, and career woman? Describe the woman. *Use present tenses in your description.*
3. In your country, are men's roles in the home changing? If so, describe how. How do you feel about these changes? Explain.
4. In your country, are women's roles in the home or at work changing? If so, describe how. How do you feel about these changes? Explain.
5. With your spouse or partner, do you share or do you expect to share the following duties: shopping for food, cooking, feeding the baby, diapering the baby, washing dishes, doing the laundry, ironing?

FOCUS 6: One-Minute Speech

- Choose one of the discussion questions above for your speech.
- Outline the points to be made.
- Time yourself at home while practicing the speech.

FOCUS 7: Write Your Opinions

- Write your opinions on any one of the discussion questions.
- Organize your ideas before writing.
- Support your opinions with specific examples.

FOCUS 8: Grammar Review

Read the following story. Circle the correct answers. Be prepared to explain your choices.

Since the 1960s, women (**are making, have been making, has made**) tremendous strides in the United States. More and more so-called (male, males) professions (**have opened, open, have open**) up to female workers. There (**is, are**) now female police officers, firefighters, and construction workers. In (the, 0) 1980s, the first woman (**was, has been, is**) appointed to the Supreme Court, the first woman (**became, has become, becomes**) an astronaut, and the first woman (**ran, has run, runs**) for vice-president. Medical schools, law schools, and business schools, which (use, used) to be predominantly male, (**are now, has now been, have now**) accepting more and more females. Recently, more women (**graduate, are graduating, have been graduating**) from college with (a, the, 0) B.A. than men. These new educational (chooses, choices) are (**lead, leading**) women into careers with (more, 0) higher salaries. In fact, the number of (females, female) lawyers and doctors (**has, have, 0**) substantially increased.

Yet, (in spite, despite) these gains, a double standard (**is still existing, still exists**) between men and women both at home and at work.

At home, although (most, most of) married women (**are working, work, have worked**), 91 percent still do all the food shopping and cooking. While the number of fathers changing diapers and taking paternity leave (**is slowly increasing, slowly increases**), child-raising falls mainly on (women, women's) shoulders. When a child (**is getting, gets**) sick, usually the mother is the one who (**is staying, stays, has stayed**) home. In fact, according to a United Nations Report, most men in the United States (**are not doing, do not do, have not done**) housework.

At work, the most visible double standard is unequal pay. Despite the Equal Pay Act, a woman (**is earning, has earned, earns**) about 70 percent of a (man, man's) salary for (the, 0) same job. Recently there (**are, have been**) lawsuits against big corporations like AT&T, General Electric, and Merrill Lynch, which were caught breaking this law and (**have paid, pay**) millions of dollars in out-of-court settlements. These successful lawsuits are (**give, given, giving**) women higher expectations.

Yet, bosses still discriminate (against, to, 0) women in hiring and promoting, and husbands (**are still holding, still hold**) back their (wives, wives') careers by not (making, doing) their share of work at home.

What (**do, are**) women (**do, doing**) now to change these inequalities? They (**have, are having**) fewer children. They (**have, are having**) children later. They (**are staying, stay**) in school longer. They (**are working, work**) longer hours. They (**speak, are speaking**) against sexual harassment on the job. They (**fight, are fighting**) for more affordable child care. They (**run, are running**) for more political offices.

The gender gap (**is shrinking, shrinks**). But for most (of, 0) women, it (**does, has, is**) not (**shrink, shrunk, shrinking**) fast enough.

▶ FOCUS 9: Dictation
....

From the tape, take a dictation. Check your writing by looking at the transcript in Appendix 2.

▶ FOCUS 10: Storytelling
....

Now it is your turn to tell members of your group a story using present tenses.

▼ From a newspaper article, a photograph, or a personal experience, find a story you want to tell.
▼ Introduce new vocabulary to your group.
▼ Limit yourself to two minutes.
▼ Tell the story without reading or memorizing it.
▼ Have your classmates retell the story in pairs.

GRAMMAR REVIEW

Present Tenses

▶ Tenses Referring to Present

There are three tenses that have different meanings and forms and represent different times in the present.

Meaning

1. The **simple present** tense refers to a *general truth* or a *repeated action*. It is often used with **adverbs of frequency** (*often, usually, generally, always, sometimes,* etc.).

    The sun **rises** in the east and **sets** in the west.

2. The **present continuous** tense stresses an *action in progress*. It also emphasizes *an action that is not permanent*. It is often used with expressions like *now, right now, at this moment, at present, currently, this week, today,* etc.

    Come quickly! The sun **is rising**.

    Note: There are some verbs (**nonaction verbs**) that are not used in the present continuous form even when they stress an action in progress. Simple present is used to indicate an ongoing action.

    The land **now belongs** to her son.

    At this moment I **believe** him.

Some of these nonaction verbs are used to express the following:

emotions: appreciate, desire, dislike, hate, like, love, need, prefer, seem, want

thoughts: believe, doubt, imagine, know, mean, recognize, remember, suppose, think, understand, wonder

measurement: cost, equal, measure, weigh

senses: appear, feel, hear, look, see, smell, taste

possession: be, belong, contain, compromise, have, include, own

Some of the verbs above can refer to an action. At that time, use present continuous. You need to think about the meaning (action versus nonaction) before selecting a verb form.

What do you think about the president now?

What are you thinking about?

Think can be an action or a nonaction verb. Look at the examples above to understand the difference in meaning. What other verbs in the nonaction list can be used as action verbs? Give examples.

3. The **present perfect** refers to an action that *started in the past* and *continues in the present.* It is often used with expressions like *since, for, up to now, so far, recently, lately,* etc.

It is now 6:00. He **has been practicing** piano for an hour.

Note that present perfect can also indicate something that occurred in the indefinite past at an unspecified time.

They **have been** to Paris.

Form

4. The simple present uses an -*s* with the third-person singular (*he, she, it*).

I/we/you/they make.

He/she/it makes.

Negatives and questions are formed using *do* or *does.*

I/we/you/they **do not make** problems.

Do I/we/you/they **make** problems?

He/she/it **does not make** problems.

Does he/she/it **make** problems?

Note that in questions and negatives there is no -s on the main verb. The -s goes on the auxiliary *do*.

5. The present continuous is formed with *am, is,* or *are* and the **present participle (-ing)** form of the verb.

I **am going.**

He/she/it **is going.**

We/they/you **are going.**

We/they/you **are going.**

Negatives and questions are formed the same way.

I **am not going.**

Am I **going?**

He/she/it **is not going.**

Is he/she/it **going?**

We/they/you **are not** going.

Are we/they/you **going?**

6. The present perfect is formed with *has* or *have* with the **past participle** of the verb (-ed for regular verbs).

He/she/it **has worked.**

I/we/you/they **have worked.**

Negatives and questions are formed in the same way.

He/she/it **has not** worked.

I/we/you **have not** worked.

Has he/she/it **worked?**

Have he/she/it **worked?**

3

Dropouts

....

Adjectives

▼ **FOCUS 1**
....

A. Meaning   Listen to the story on the tape. What is the main idea? With a partner, write two or three sentences that best summarize the main idea.

B. Vocabulary   Do you understand the italicized words below? If not, listen to the story on the tape. Try to understand what the following words mean after hearing them in the story. Can you guess the correct meaning? What words or sentences help you guess? Explain to a partner or your group members what you think these words mean.

one out of four	*proponents*	*drawings*
revoke	*opponents*	*trend*
incentive	*Federal grant*	

▼ **FOCUS 2: Adjectives**
....

A. The story you have just heard uses many adjective and noun combinations. Notice how adjectives do *not* change when used with a plural noun.

This is **their car**. These are **their cars**.

He brought **the other book**. He brought **the other books**.

Some words can be nouns and adjectives. But as adjectives they do not take *-s*.

He is **ten years old**. He is a **ten-year-old** boy.

That hat cost **ten dollars**. It's a **ten-dollar** hat.

Practice: Tell the age of all your relatives, using combined adjectives.

Example

I have an eighty-year-old grandmother.

B. Edit   Read the sentence below. Look for errors in adjective forms. Make the necessary corrections.

> If they bring theirs supplies to school, they will receive five dollars a day, which means a twenty-five dollars check a week.

C. Listen   Now listen to the story again. List as many adjectives as you can hear.

▼ FOCUS 3: Retell the Story

In pairs or as a class, retell the story you have just heard. Your instructor will stop you when you make a mistake. The next student corrects and continues the story.

▼ FOCUS 4: Write the Story

Write a summary of the story in your own words. Be sure to check the adjective forms.

Dropping Out

Reasons students give in the United States for not completing high school:

boredom	pregnancy
emotional problems	grades
marriage	finances
work	fear of violence

1. Which of the above reasons do you find surprising? Explain why.

2. Why do you think people drop out of high school in your country?

▼ FOCUS 5: Discuss the Story

Discuss the following questions with group members.

1. Do you think giving money, revoking driver's licenses, or giving work-study programs will alleviate the dropout problem? Explain why any of the above will or will not work.

2. What do you think is a good method to prevent the high dropout rate?

3. If you were the judge in West Virginia, how would you rule in the sixteen-year-old boy's case? Give reasons.

4. Is there a dropout problem in your country? Describe the situation.

5. Have you ever felt like dropping out of school? Explain.

6. In some states in the United States, a fifteen-year-old can get a driver's license. How does this compare to your country?

▼ FOCUS 6: One-Minute Speech

▼ Choose one of the discussion questions above for your speech.
▼ Outline the points to be made.
▼ Time yourself at home while practicing the speech.

▼ FOCUS 7: Write Your Opinions

▼ Write your opinions on any one of the discussion questions.
▼ Organize your ideas before writing.
▼ Support your opinions with specific examples.

▼ FOCUS 8: Grammar Review

Read the following story. Circle the correct answers. Be prepared to explain your choices.

In West Virginia and in New York, one out of four students (drop, drops) out (of, off, from, 0) high school. In Washington, DC, the statistics (is, are) even (**worst, worse**). One half of all high (**schools, school**) students never graduate. Nationwide, (an, 0, the) overall dropout rate is 29 percent. Many say they drop out because they are (**bored, boring**). Because of this, U.S. educators (try, are trying, has been trying) to figure out (a, the, 0) way to stop this (**disturbed, disturbing**) trend. In Chicago, some schools (throw, are throwing) pizza parties for (**potential, potentials**) dropouts. In Milwaukee, some schools are having lotteries for (**use, used, useds**) cars for students who stay in school. In Philadelphia, at-risk students are being (award, awarding, awarded) after- (**schools, school**) jobs and (**summers, summer**) jobs for staying in school. But in a New Jersey high school, one (principle, principal) is using money, not jobs, as (an, a, 0) incentive.

This school received a hundred-thousand- (**dollar, dollars**) grant to pay students (who, which, 0) are at risk of dropping out. When (**this, these**) students go to class on time, bring (**their, theirs**) notebooks, and (make, do) their (homeworks, homework), they make five (**dollars, dollar**) a day. This means students can bring home a (**twenty-five-dollars, twenty-five-dollar**) check every week for (assisting, attending) classes five days in a row. While the program is new, the (principal, principle) claims that he has (all ready, already) achieved (a, the, 0) higher rate of attendance with (**this, these**) money incentive. But some say (it, 0) is (too, so, very) early to talk about the program's (succeed, success, successful). Still (**the others, others, other**) feel that even if it does work, using money as (an, the, 0) incentive is wrong. There are (**severals, several**) programs (as, like) this one to keep (**uninterested, uninteresting**) students in school.

West (**Virginian, virginian**) educators, however, have taken a (dif-

ferent, difference) approach. Instead (to pay, of paying) students, they (decide, have decided, had decided) to revoke a (student, student's, students') driver's license when the student stops (to go, going, go) to class. But this ruling is now (0, being, been) challenged by a sixteen- (**year-old, years-old**) boy. He said that he (has, have, had) to quit (go, going, to go) to school because he got his fifteen- (**year-old, years-old**) girlfriend (**pregnant, pregnancy**). To support (his, her) new wife, he said he (need, needed, needs) to drive (a, the) car. Now the court (decides, is deciding, has deciding) what to do in this case. Meanwhile, (**the others, other, others**) states have enacted (**similar, similars**) laws. Proponents of (**this, these**) laws say that students cannot understand that dropping out of school means a (**low-paid, low-paying**) job, but they can understand what (does it mean, it means) not to be able to drive. However, opponents of this law feel that a school may (success, succeed) in getting students (to stay, stay, staying) in school but it cannot make (him, them, him or her) (learn, to learn, learning). If students are not (**interested, interesting**) in learning, they will not learn.

FOCUS 9: Dictation

From the tape, take a dictation. Check your writing by looking at the transcript in Appendix 2.

FOCUS 10: Storytelling

Now it is your turn to tell members of your group a story using adjective forms.

▶ From a newspaper article, a photograph, or a personal experience, find a story you want to tell.

▶ Introduce new vocabulary to your group.

▶ Limit yourself to two minutes.

▶ Tell the story without reading or memorizing it.

▶ Have your classmates retell the stories in pairs.

GRAMMAR REVIEW
Adjectives

▶ Adjectives

1. An adjective modifies a noun or pronoun.

   Emile is a **beautiful** baby.

   He is **beautiful**.

2. Never put an *-s* or a plural ending on an **adjective**. Study the following changes.

a trip of six hours	a **six-hour** trip
an essay of five hundred words	a **five-hundred-word** essay
a ceiling of ten feet	a **ten-foot** ceiling

3. Change *this* and *that* to *these* and *those* when the noun is plural.

this politician	**these** politicians
that senator	**those** senators

4. Avoid confusing the pronoun *others* and *the others* with the adjectives *other* and *the other*.

   Let's go to the party with **the other** students.

   Let's go to the party with **the others**.

5. Choose the right ending (suffix) for an adjective. Cover up the right column below. Change the nouns into adjectives, then study the changes. Think of other adjectives with similar endings.

Noun Forms	*Adjective Forms*
difference	different
guilt	guilty
trouble	troublesome
anxiety	anxious
success	successful
war	warlike
sense	sensible
cost	costly
child	childish, childlike, childless
father	fatherless, fatherly
impression	impressive
economy	economic, economical
politics	political
scare	scary
globe	global
belief	believable
pregnancy	pregnant
America	American

Note: The same root word can have different adjective endings. This changes the meaning of the word. Check adjectives with different forms in your dictionary. Try to explain the different nuances in meaning. When in doubt about an adjective form, use a dictionary.

6. Be careful when choosing an *-ing* or *-ed* ending. Use *-ing* for adjectives when **active** in meaning (the subject is equal to the adjective: *The movie is boring. the movie = boring*). Use *-ed* for adjectives when passive in meaning (the subject receives the action: *They are bored by the movie. the movie = bores them*). Study the difference in meanings between the following sentences.

He is **bored** by the teacher. (This means the teacher puts him to sleep.) The teacher is **boring.**

He is **boring to talk to.** (This means other people are put to sleep by him.) They are **bored by him** when he talks.

7. Capitalize adjectives of origin (city, state, nation).

> Is this **Japanese** food?
>
> Where is the **American** restaurant?
>
> The singer is **Parisian**.

8. Use adjectives with the verbs *be, become, feel, look, smell, sound,* and *taste* when the verb *be* can be substituted. Study the difference in meaning in these sentences. Then make your own sentences to show the difference.

> She **looks angry**.
>
> She **looked at the officer angrily**.

8. Note the irregular forms of the comparisons below.

Positive	*Comparative*	*Superlative*
bad	worse	worst
far	farther*	farthest
far	further*	furthest
good	better	best
little	less	least
many	more	most
much	more	most

*Farther describes distances, whereas *further* describes time or quantity. *You throw a ball* **farther.** *You want to study adjectives* **further.**

4

Wrong Side of the Bed

....

Verbs of Perception
Articles

FOCUS 1

A. Meaning Listen to the story on the tape. What is the main idea? With a partner, write two or three sentences that best summarize the main idea.

B. Vocabulary Do you understand the italicized words below? If not, listen to the story on the tape again. Try to understand what the following words mean after hearing them in the story. Can you guess the correct meaning? What words or sentences help you guess? Explain to a partner or your group members what you think these words mean.

got up on the wrong side of the bed	*grabbed onto*
paranoid	*tore off*
robbed	*bewildered*

FOCUS 2: Verbs of Perception

A. The story you have just heard has many verbs of perception: *see, watch, notice, feel,* and *hear*. These verbs are followed by the gerund form (*-ing*) or the base form (without *to*).

Example

I **heard** him **sing.** I **heard** him **singing.**

Say aloud the following sentences, putting the verb in the correct form.

1. At school I saw him (run) ________ around all day long.

2. At the gym he watches me (run) ________ every week.

3. What did you hear her (say) ________ ?

4. If you notice him (come) ________ in, tell me.

B. Edit Read the sentences below. Look for errors in verb forms. Make the necessary corrections.

1. While the train was speeding down the tracks, he felt a man bumped into him.

2. He saw the man got off.

C. **Listen** Now listen to the story again. List as many verbs of perception as you hear.

FOCUS 3: Retell the Story

In pairs or as a class, retell the story you have just heard. Your instructor will stop you when you make a mistake. The next student corrects and continues the story.

FOCUS 4: Write the Story

Write a summary of the story in your own words. Be sure to check the verb forms, especially after the verbs of perception.

FOCUS 5: Discuss the Story

Discuss the following questions with group members.

1. When an American notices someone staring at him or her, what can he or she do or say? When an American bumps into someone by accident, what is said? What would you or someone from your country say or do in those situations?
2. Have you ever been suspected of doing something that you had not done? Tell what happened.
3. Have you ever accused someone of doing something and then found out later that you had made a mistake? Explain what happened.

4. Have you ever had something stolen from you? Explain what happened and how you felt. Try to use the verbs *feel*, *hear*, *notice*, *observe*, *overhear*, *see*, and *watch* in your answer.

5. What types of warnings did your friends, relatives, and newspapers give you about coming to the United States? Use this structure when answering.

   My friend **warned me about how** expensive the dormitory **would be.**

   What types of warnings would you give to an American going to your country? For example:

   I would warn him or her about how expensive public transportation is.

FOCUS 6: One-Minute Speech

- Choose one of the discussion questions above for your speech.
- Outline the points to be made.
- Time yourself at home while practicing the speech.

FOCUS 7: Write Your Opinions

- Write your opinions on any one of the discussion questions.
- Organize your ideas before writing.
- Support your opinions with specific examples.

FOCUS 8: Grammar in Review

A. Read the following story. Circle the correct answers. Be prepared to explain your choices.

This is a story about (a, an, the) eighteen- (years, year) -old foreign student who didn't hear his alarm clock (**ring, rang, to ring**) so he (wake, woke) up (a, an) hour late for school. Because he was late, he just (throw, through, threw) on some clothes and (**run, ran**) out of the house. (What, What a, How) a terrible mood he was in! He really (fell, felt) he had gotten up on the wrong side of (his, the) bed.

He (run, ran) down the stairs (into, onto) the subway platform. While waiting for the train, he picked (up, out, 0) a newspaper he saw (**lying, laying**) on the bench. After a ten- (minutes, minute) wait, the train arrived (in, at) the station. He got onto the (crowd, crowded, crowding) train. While the train (sped, was speeding) down the tracks, he felt a man (**to bump, bumped, bumping**) into him. He thought that (the, a, 0) same man had been watching him (**to read, read**) his newspaper (in, on, at) the subway platform. All (a, of, of a) sudden, he (feel, fell, felt) afraid. He remembered how his family (warned, were warning, had warned) him about how dangerous (was the United States, the United States was). He didn't think that he was (0, being, been) paranoid. He thought he (was, was being, has been) robbed.

Sure enough, when the student (put, has put, had put) his hand inside his bag, his wallet was gone. Just then the train (stoped, stopped). He saw the man (**to get, got, getting**) off. The student shouted, "Stop! Thief! He stole my wallet!" Immediately, (most of, the most, most of the) passengers (near, near to) the door grabbed onto the (man, man's) jacket. Just then the doors of the subway train (shutted, shut). The man looked (shock, shocked, shocking) as the passengers tore off his sleeve. As the train pulled out of the station, the young man (was breaking, broke, has broken) down into tears about his (lost, loss, loose) wallet. Some of (the, a, 0) passengers, (felt, feeling) sorry for the bewildered student, took up a small collection for him so that he could get to (a, the, 0) school.

When the student arrived home that evening, he was (so, such, very, too) sad to think. As he walked toward his bed, he felt even (more sad, sadder, saddest). There on the table (close, near, near to, nearby) his bed, he saw his wallet. He couldn't believe (what, what a, how) terrible mistake he had made. Never again (he would, would he) leave his house when he was in (so, such, such a) mood. What would he say if he ever saw that man (**stood, to stand, standing**) at that subway station again?

B. **Review in Articles**   Add *a, an,* or *the* to the story below. When in doubt, check the rules on articles in the Grammar Review at the end of the chapter.

This is story about eighteen-year-old foreign student who didn't hear his alarm clock ring so he woke up hour late for school. Because he was late, he just threw on some clothes and ran out of house. What terrible mood he was in! He really felt he had gotten up on wrong side of bed.

He ran down stairs onto subway platform. While waiting for train, he picked up newspaper he saw lying on bench. After ten-minute wait, train arrived at station. He got onto crowded train. While train was speeding down tracks, he felt man bumping into him. He thought that same man had been watching him read his newspaper on subway platform. All of sudden, he felt afraid. He remembered how his family had warned him about how dangerous United States was. He didn't think he was being paranoid. He thought he was being robbed.

Sure enough, when student put his hand inside his bag, his wallet was gone. Just then train stopped. He saw man getting off. Student shouted, "Stop! Thief! He stole my wallet!" Immediately, most of passengers near the door grabbed onto man's jacket. Just then doors of subway train shut. Man looked shocked as passengers tore off his sleeve. As train pulled out of station, young man broke down into tears about his lost wallet. Some of passengers, feeling sorry for bewildered student, took up small collection for him so that he could get to school.

▶ FOCUS 9: Dictation

From the tape, take a dictation. Check your writing by looking at the transcript in Appendix 2.

▶ FOCUS 10: Storytelling

Now it is your turn to tell members of your group a story using verbs of perception.

▶ From a newspaper article, a photograph, or a personal experience, find a story you want to tell.
▶ Introduce new vocabulary to your group.
▶ Limit yourself to two minutes.
▶ Tell the story without reading or memorizing it.
▶ Have your classmates retell the story in pairs.

GRAMMAR REVIEW

Verbs of Perception
Articles

▶ Verbs of Perception

1. Following these verbs of perception, *feel, hear, listen to, notice, observe, overhear, see,* and *watch,* use the infinitive (base with form *to*) or gerund form (base form with *-ing*) of the verb.

   I **overheard** him **whispering** about me.

   I **saw** them **leave** their house yesterday.

   I **see** them **leave** their house every day.

   I **will listen to** her **practicing** her speech.

2. In the examples above, note how the verb tense (present, past, or future) is *not* reflected in the verb following a verb of perception.

3. Use only the gerund form following *smell* and *find.*

   I **smelled** the pie **burning.**

   I **found** the boy **crying.**

▶ Articles

1. An **article** is a word that comes before a noun and usually tells whether the noun is something general or specific. English has three articles: *a,*

an, and *the*. To use articles correctly, you need to learn about **countable** and **uncountable nouns.**

2. Nouns can be countable or uncountable or either depending on meaning. Uncountable nouns are usually more nonspecific and less concrete. They cannot be counted as a single unit or item. Countable nouns are more concrete. They can be counted.

3. Singular countable nouns take *a* or *an* when the meaning is "one" or "any." Note whether or not the following common nouns are countable.

Countable	*Uncountable*
a suitcase	luggage
a bag	baggage
a letter	mail
a painting	art
an insult	discrimination
a word	vocabulary
an assignment	homework
a problem	trouble
a machine	machinery
an advertisement	advertising
a chair	furniture
a stereo	audio equipment
a jam	traffic
a suggestion	advice
a climate	weather
a concert	music
a game	tennis
a clue	evidence
a cigarette	smoking
a fact	information
a dollar	money
a fact	knowledge
a job	work
a news item	news
a sock	underwear
a cow	beef, cattle
a landing	land
a roll of film	film

4. *An* is used for nouns that start with a *vowel sound.*

> She received **an M.B.A.** from Harvard.

> I'll meet you in **an hour.**

> They started **a union.**

> He is looking for **an umbrella.**

5. Many nouns can be either countable or uncountable. However, the meaning of the word changes. Note the differences in meanings in the following sentences.

> He had ten years of nursing **experience.** (Here *experience* is knowledge or skill.)

> He had **a good experience** at the hospital. (Here *experience* is an activity.)

> **Abortion** is a controversial topic. (Here *abortion* is an issue.)

> She had **an abortion** last week. (Here *abortion* is an act.)

6. Use *the* to denote a specific noun. All nouns (countable, uncountable, singular, and plural) can take *the.*

> I bought **the** dress you liked. (The *the* denotes a specific dress—not any one.)

> **The** Japanese government is changing its trade regulations. (The *the* denotes a specific government, not any government.)

7. Note that uncountable nouns with adjectives remain general classification unless they are made more specific.

> I love to listen to classical music. (Here *classical music* represents a general classification of a type of music, so *the* is not used.)

> I love to listen to the classical music of Bach. (Here *classical music* is made specific with the word *of;* use *the.*)

8. Expressions with *of* usually take *the.*

> the Museum of Modern Art

> the University of Hawaii

> the United States of America

9. *Most,* *most of the,* *almost,* and *the most* are often confused. Note the differences in the following sentences.

> Most people vote. (This sentence refers to most people in general, so *the* is not used).

> Most of the people in my class voted. (This sentence refers to a specific group of people, so *the* is used.)

> Almost all the people in my class voted. (*Almost,* meaning "nearly," acts as an adverb. *The* is used because this sentence refers to a specific group of people.)

> This was the most unusual election. (Superlatives take *the.*)

10. Using the article *the* can be especially confusing with some of the common expressions listed below. Examine the list to see how similar expressions may or may not require a *the.*

the United States	America
the East River	Lake George
the Atlantic Ocean	Chesapeake Bay
the Lincoln Tunnel	Lincoln Street
the Avenue of the Americas	Sixth Avenue
the Long Island Expressway	Route 25
the Golden Gate Bridge	bridges
the E train	trains
the Second World War	World War II
the Everglades	Central Park
the fifth chapter	Fifth Avenue
the English language	English*
the president of the United States	President Jefferson
the United Kingdom	Great Britain
the Bronx	Manhattan
the death penalty	capital punishment

*English refers to the language; but *the English* means the people of England.

the Smiths	Mary Smith
the same as	as much as
the police	police officers
the army	soldiers
the *New York Times*	*Time* magazine

11. *The* is also used in the following situations:

▼ When the noun refers to something *unique*

   the sky

▼ When the noun is known to speaker and listener

   I'll take the dog for a walk.

▼ When the noun is countable, signifying all of a species

   The dog is a popular pet in the United States.

▼ When adjectives are used as nouns

the poor	the unemployed
the homeless	the young

12. Memorize idioms. When in doubt, consult a dictionary. Some common idioms are:

   go to court, jail, prison, heaven, hell, bed, school, work, and church

   in the evening, in the morning, at night

   at the time, in time, a long time ago

5

Drunk Driving

························

Passive Voice

Ever Get A Pal Smashed?

TAKE THE KEYS.
CALL A CAB.
TAKE A STAND.

FRIENDS DON'T LET FRIENDS DRIVE DRUNK

Ad U.S. Department of Transportation

DRUNK DRIVING PREVENTION CAMPAIGN
MAGAZINE AD NO. DD-2843-90—7" x 10" (110 Screen)
Volunteer Agency: Wells, Rich, Greene, Inc., Campaign Director: Richard S. Helstein, General Foods, USA

Test Your Knowledge

Directions: Mark the following statements true or false. Then check your answers at the bottom of the page.

1. Black coffee, cold showers, and walking around outdoors will help make a person sober.

2. A full stomach will keep a person from getting drunk.

3. A person who has had six beers will not have traces of alcohol in his or her blood six hours later.

4. Beer or wine is less likely to make a person drunk than so-called hard drinks.

Answers: 1. F; 2. F; 3. F; 4. F. All answers are based on customer information from General Motors.

▼ FOCUS 1

A. Meaning   Listen to the story on the tape. What is the main idea? With a partner, write two or three sentences that best summarize the main idea.

B. Vocabulary   Do you understand the italicized words below? If not, listen to the story on the tape again. Try to understand what the following words mean after hearing them in the story. Can you guess the correct meaning? What words or sentences help you guess? Explain to a partner or your group members what you think these words mean.

ran through	*crashed into*
struck	*indicted*
harshly	*suspended*
revoked	

▼ FOCUS 2: Passive Voice

A. Passive voice is used when the receiver of an action is more important than the doer. To form the passive voice, use the verb *to be* (in the correct verb tense) and **the past participle** of the verb (base form plus -*ed*). For irregular verbs, check the list on pages 12–14.

Example

The Senate **passes** anti–drunk-driving laws every year. (The passive form is: Every year anti–drunk-driving laws *are passed*.)

Now say aloud to your neighbor the passive form of the following sentences.

The Senate is passing an anti–drunk-driving law now.

The Senate passed an anti–drunk-driving law last year.

The Senate will pass an anti–drunk-driving law next month.

The Senate has just passed an anti–drunk-driving law.

Before the accident occurred, the Senate had passed an anti–drunk-driving law.

If the Senate were realistic, it would pass an anti–drunk-driving law.

If the Senate had not gone on vacation early, it would have passed an anti–drunk-driving law.

B. Edit   Read the sentences below. Look for errors in the passive voice. Make the necessary corrections.

1. The car was been driven by a mother.

2. All of the passengers were kill.

C. Listen   Now listen to the story again. Try to list as many verbs in the passive voice as you hear.

▶FOCUS 3: Retell the Story
....

In pairs or as a class, retell the story you have just heard. Your instructor will stop you when you make a mistake. The next student corrects and continues the story.

▶FOCUS 4: Write the Story
....

Write a summary of the story in your own words. Be sure to check the passive-voice forms.

....

Views of Americans on Restrictions of Alcoholic Beverages*

	Yes	No
Require warning labels about the dangers of alcohol	67%	16
Have alcoholic beverage companies contribute $1 to	58	25

	Yes	No
charity for every $14 of sales	58	25
Ban all ads for beer and wine from television	48	31
Eliminate ads for liquor from magazines and newspapers	42	34
Prevent bars from selling a patron more than one drink per hour	35	43
Outlaw alcoholic beverages	15	69

*Source: Based on "Rebelling against Alcohol, Tobacco Ads," in the *Wall Street Journal* 14 Nov. 1989.

Compare your views to those of Americans in the above survey. Explain your reasoning. Use the passive voice in your answers. For example: *Warning labels should (not) be required because . . .*

FOCUS 5: Discuss the Story

Discuss the following questions with group members.

1. What would have happened to the thirty-year-old drunk driver if he had had the accident in your country? Would his license have been revoked or suspended? Would he have been arrested? Would he have been given a heavy or light sentence? Would he have been looked down upon by society? *Use passive voice in your answer.*
2. How should the thirty-year-old driver have been sentenced? Explain why. *Use passive voice in your answer.*
3. Have you or anyone you know ever been in a car accident? Was your car damaged? Were you injured? Was anybody else hurt? Were you fined? Were you arrested? Was there any other property damage? Was your license taken away? Explain what happened.
4. In Maine, a passenger who allowed a drunken person to drive his truck was convicted as an accomplice to the crime of driving under the influence of alcohol. What do you think of this ruling?

5. In Florida, a mother won an $800,000 suit against an employer who allowed her son to drive home after serving him alcohol at a business social gathering. He died in a car accident. What do you think of this ruling?

▼ FOCUS 6: One-Minute Speech

▼ Choose one of the discussion questions above for your speech.
▼ Outline the points to be made.
▼ Time yourself at home while practicing the speech.

▼ FOCUS 7: Write Your Opinions

▼ Write your opinions on any one of the discussion questions.
▼ Organize your ideas before writing.
▼ Support your opinions with specific examples.

▼ FOCUS 8: Grammar Review

Read the following story. Circle the correct answers. Be prepared to explain your choices.

The United States has one of the lowest (rate, rates) of car accidents in the world. Yet, every year about (44,000, 44.000) people (die, died, are dying) on the highways in (cars, car) accidents in the United States. Half of (this, these) (dead, deads, deaths) are (**causing, cause, caused**) by (drunk, drunks) drivers. Because of this, (strictest, stricter, more strict) laws (**are passed, are passing, have been passed**) recently. California has one of the (most strict, strictest) laws. This law states that if you kill someone while you are driving (**intoxicate, intoxicated**), you will (**consider, be considered, be consider**) a (murder, murderer) in the eyes of the law. This is a story about what happened to (a, 0, the) thirty- (years, year) -old man in California.

One afternoon this man (drinks, drank, drunk, drunken) four bottles of beer at (a, the, 0) bar. After (to finish, finished, finishing) his drinks, he got (into, onto, on) his car and (drive, drove) (of, off). He was speeding. He (run, ran) (through, into, at) a stop sign and crashed (through, into, to, at) another car (crossed, crossing, cross) the intersection. He didn't have enough time (to stop, for stopping). The car that was (**strike, struck, stricken**) was (**been, being**) driven by a mother; inside were her four children. All of the passengers (**was killed, were kill, were killed**). However, the drunk driver (**didn't injure, wasn't injured**) at all. When (a, the, 0) police (**was, were, 0**) arrived, (he, they) arrested the driver and (bringing, brought) him to court. There he was (**indict, indicted**) for murder. After a two- (months, month) trial, he was (**found, find, founded**) guilty of murder. He was (**sentence, sentenced**) to seventy-seven years in prison. While some (feel, fell, feels) his sentence was (**justify, justified, justifying**), others feel he was (**sentence, sentencing, sentenced**) (to, too) harshly because he had not planned the accident. However, those (in, on) favor of the sentence said this was not (the, 0) first time he (**has been, had been, was**) arrested for drunk driving. (The last, Last) time he had his (driver, driver's) license (**suspending, suspend, suspended**) for six (months, month). This time his license has been (**revoke, revoking, revoked**) for life.

▼ FOCUS 9: Dictation
....

From the tape, take a dictation. Check your writing by looking at the transcript in Appendix 2.

▼ FOCUS 10: Storytelling

Now it is your turn to tell members of your group a story using the passive voice.

▼ From a newspaper article, a photograph, or a personal experience, find a story you want to tell.
▼ Introduce new vocabulary to your group.
▼ Limit yourself to two minutes.
▼ Tell the story without reading or memorizing it.
▼ Have your classmates retell the story in pairs.

GRAMMAR REVIEW

· · · · · · · · · · · · · · · · ·

Passive Voice

▶ The Passive Voice

1. Use **passive voice** when the doer is not as important as the receiver.

   President Kennedy was shot.

   The president is more important than the person who shot him.

2. Use passive voice when you do not want to mention the doer.

   It is said that there was a conspiracy behind the assassination.

3. Use passive voice only with verbs that take direct objects (transitive verbs) and never with verbs that do not take direct objects (intransitive verbs). Note that *appear, arrive, be, die, grow up, happen, occur, seem,* and *rise* are *never* used in the passive voice.

   He **died** of a stroke.

   He **was killed** by a stroke.

   It **happened** suddenly.

   It **was brought about** by unknown causes.

   She **grew** up in the country.

   She **was raised** by her uncle in the country.

4. The passive voice is formed with the verb *to be* and the past participle of the verb.

   A test is being prepared now. (present continuous)

A test is prepared every year. (simple present)

A test was prepared yesterday. (simple past)

A test has recently been prepared. (present perfect)

A test will be prepared next week. (future)

A test is going to be prepared soon. (future)

A test could have been prepared. (past conditional)

A test would have been prepared. (past conditional)

A test should have been prepared. (past modal)

A test may have been prepared. (past modal)

5. Avoid using the passive voice unnecessarily. Conciseness and directness are the best forms in writing.

> When **her book was read by her father,** she was proud. (wordy, heavy style)

> While **her father read her book,** she was proud. (concise and clear style)

6. There is a passive form with *get* and *have* (causative verbs) that does not use the verb *to be.*

> She **got hired by** the president. (This means she was hired. The president hired her.)

> She **had her paper typed by** the secretary. (This means the secretary was asked by her to type it.)

7. When using the passive voice, do not confuse *been* with *being. Been* follows the verb *to have,* and *being* follows the verb *to be.*

> His competence **is being** challenged.

> His competence **has been** challenged.

6

The Police Commissioner's Advice

··

Causatives
Suggest and *Recommend*

▼ FOCUS 1

A. Meaning   Listen to the story on the tape. What is the main idea? With a partner, write two or three sentences that best summarize the main idea.

B. Vocabulary   Do you understand the italicized words below? If not, listen to the story on the tape. Try to understand what the following words mean after hearing them in the story. Can you guess the correct meaning? What words or sentences help you guess? Explain to a partner or your group members what you think these words mean.

smash	*snore*	*grunt*
vandalism	*broke into*	*greet*
commissioner		

▼ FOCUS 2: Causatives and *Suggest* and *Recommend*

A. Causatives—Active Voice   The story you have just heard uses causative verbs—*make, let,* and *have.* Notice how the verb following a causative verb is in the base form (no *to* and no *-ing)* in active voice.

He's **letting** me **use** his computer.

The teacher **made** us **type** our homework.

What will she **have** them **bring** to the party?

B. Causative—Passive Voice   The verb following a causative verb is a past participle.

I **had** my daughter **wash** the car. (active voice)

I **had** the car **washed.** (passive voice)

Now tell your neighbor five things you had someone do. Then change those sentences to the passive voice by telling your neighbor what you had done.

C. *Suggest* **and** *Recommend*   When *suggest* and *recommend* are used to mean "should," the verb following *suggest* or *recommend* is in the base form.

> I suggest (am suggesting, suggested, will suggest) that he **be** here on time. (This means he *should be here on time,* but in formal English, *should* is not used.)

> To form the negative, add *not.* Never use *do, does,* or *did* to form a negative after these verbs.

> I suggest (am suggesting, suggested, will suggest) that he **not be** late. (This means he *should not be* late.)

> Now with your partner, make recommendations and suggestions about what an American should see or not see when visiting your country or city.

> I recommend that he or she visit Central Park. I suggest that he or she not go there after dark.

D. Edit   Read the following sentences. Look for errors in verb forms. Make the necessary corrections.

1. The homeless man said that the psychologist should have someone to watch his car for him.

2. He hadn't had his car windows smash.

3. The repairman recommended that he parks his car in a garage.

E. Listen   Now listen to the story again. Try to list as many causative verbs as you hear.

▶ FOCUS 3: Retell the Story

In pairs or as a class, retell the story you have just heard. Your instructor will stop you when you make a mistake. The next student corrects and continues the story.

▼ FOCUS 4: Write the Story

Write a summary of the story in your own words. Be sure to check the verb forms following causative verbs.

Got an idea?
Send it to us

You can help make New York a safer place.

Join the Daily News Crimefighter campaign. Send us your idea on fighting crime. Every day, we'll award $25 for the best crimefighting suggestion. Maybe your tip will help save a life, prevent a burglary, foil a stickup or avoid an injury.

Please do not telephone. Write your idea in 50 words or less.

Mail it to:

CRIMEFIGHTER
P.O. Box 1481
Grand Central Station
New York, N.Y. 10017

TODAY'S WINNER
Fran Aiello
Queens

The Idea

Burglars don't like to enter homes while the occupants are inside. So if you leave your home, make it appear someone is there. Keep a rug or some towels on the clothesline at all times.*

*Source: (N.Y.) *Daily News*.

Write your idea on fighting crime in fifty words or less. Students will vote on which suggestion is best. Trying using causative verbs in your response.

▼ FOCUS 5: Discuss the Story

Discuss the following questions with group members.

1. Is there a problem of vandalism in your country or where you live? If so, describe the situation. How can you make people respect other people's property?

2. What do you suggest that the psychologist do to prevent vandalism to his car?

3. Is there a problem of homelessness in your country? Describe the situation.

4. What do you suggest that a government do to prevent homelessness?

▼ FOCUS 6: One-Minute Speech

▼ Choose one of the discussion questions above for your speech.
▼ Outline the points to be made.
▼ Time yourself at home while practicing the speech.

▼ FOCUS 7: Write Your Opinions

▼ Write your opinions on any one of the discussion questions.
▼ Organize your ideas before writing.
▼ Support your opinions with specific examples.

▼ FOCUS 8: Grammar Review

Read the following story. Circle the correct answers. Be prepared to explain your choices.

A psychologist (lived, living) in the city was (very, too) tired of having his car (**break, broke, broken, breaking**) into every (month, months). Typically, someone looking for a radio to steal (will, would) smash a window. To have a car window (**replace, replaced, replacing**) would end up costing a hundred dollars. After having a repairman (**to fix, fixed, fixing, fix**) his last window, the psychologist was (determine, determined) to do something about this vandalism. The repairman recommended that he (**park, parks, parked**) his car in a garage and that he (**does, did, 0**) never leave it on the street. The psychologist, however, (fell, felt) a garage would be too expensive. That night, (in, on, at) the newspaper, he read a (news, news item) about the police (commissioner, commissioner's) (advice, advise) on car vandalism. It seems that the commissioner had the same problem (**happened, to happen, happen, happening**) to him. He suggested that (cars, car) owners (**leave, leaving, left**) the doors unlocked so a thief (can, could) see that there was (anything, nothing) to steal. He also recommended that a person (**do, did, 0**) not leave anything of value in the car. The police commissioner wrote that since he started this method, he hadn't had his car windows (**smash, smashed, smashing**) nor (he had, had he) had his car locks (**broke, breaking, broken**). The psychologist thought it was important that he (**followed, follows, follow**) the commissioner's advice.

A week after trying this new method, the psychologist had (a, the, 0) big surprise. At 8:00 A.M., he went (to, 0) downstairs to (live, leave) for work. When he arrived (to, at, in) the car, all the doors (was, were) locked. He couldn't understand what (is, was) going on. He was (very, so, too) sure that he had left his doors (unlocked, unlock). Finally, when he unlocked the door, he noticed that the front seat (pull, pulled, was pulled) forward. Also, although he didn't smoke, (but, 0) the car smelled of cigarettes. Suddenly, the psychologist was taken aback when he (heared, heard, hears) a grunt from (a, the, 0) back (sit, set, seat). There was a man in (the, his) sixties snoring away. Looking at the homeless man, the psychologist didn't know what to do. Should he let him (**sleep, to sleep, sleeping**)? Because the psychologist had to go to work, he decided he (must, has, had) to wake him up. The psychologist greeted the homeless man. As he opened his eyes, the homeless man wanted to know what time (is it, was it, it is, it was). The psychologist told him that he was (in, on) his way to work and he (will, would) drop him (0, off, out) somewhere. The homeless man replied that he (has, had) nowhere to go so he (will, would) get (out, off) there. Before leaving, the homeless man suggested that he (**has, had, have**) someone (**watched, to watch, watching, watch**) his car so that nobody would steal it. As the old man got (off, out, out of) the car, the psychologist thanked the man for his (advices, advise, advice).

▼ FOCUS 9: Dictation

From the tape, take a dictation. Check your writing by looking at the transcript in Appendix 2.

▼ FOCUS 10: Storytelling

Now it is your turn to tell members of your group a story using the active and passive form of causative verbs.

▼ From a newspaper article, a photograph, or a personal experience, find a story you want to tell.
▼ Introduce new vocabulary to your group.
▼ Limit yourself to two minutes.
▼ Tell the story without reading or memorizing it.
▼ Have your classmates retell the stories in pairs.

GRAMMAR REVIEW

. . . .

Causatives
Suggest and *Recommend*

▶ **Causatives**

. . . .

1. *Make, let,* and *have* are called **causatives** when they "cause" something to happen.

2. Use the base form of the verb after the causative appears.

   She **has** her husband **pick** her up from work every day.

   Note that the verb following the causative *never* changes its form no matter what tense the causative verb is in.

   Yesterday he **had** her husband **pick** her up from work.

3. Never use an infinitive *(to* plus base) or gerund *(-ing* form) following *make, let,* and *have.*

4. Do not confuse present perfect or past perfect tenses with causatives.

   I **have washed** the car recently.

   I **had washed** the car before it rained.

   I **had** my daughter **wash** the car.

5. The passive form of the causative is used when the doer is unknown or unimportant. Note that the past participle, not the base form, is used following the object.

   I **had** the car **washed.** (Who washed the car is unimportant.)

▼ *Suggest* and *Recommend*

1. When ***suggest*** and ***recommend*** express "urgency" or "necessity," they are often followed by a *that* clause with the base form (infinitive without *to*) as its verb. This structure appears more in formal English.

    I **recommend that** he **go.**

2. The following are other verbs that express "urgency" and "necessity" like *suggest* and *recommend* and follow the same pattern.

*advise	*direct	**propose
arrange	*forbid	**recommend
*ask	insist	*request
*beg	intend	require
*command	move	stipulate
demand	*order	**suggest
*desire	**prefer	*urge

    The verbs marked with (*) can also be followed by an infinitive.

    I begged **that he go.**

    I begged **him to go.**

    The verbs marked with (**) can also be followed by a gerund.

    I suggest **that he go.**

    I suggest (**his**) **going.**

    See the Grammar Review on gerunds in Chapter 8.

2. While the main verb can change tenses, the verb in the *that* clause never changes.

    I suggest**ed** that he **go.**

    I **will** suggest that he **go.**

    I **would have suggested** that he **go.**

    I **am suggesting** that he **go.**

3. To form the negative of the verb in the *that* clause, only add *not*.

   I suggest that he **not go.**

   He asked that we **not be** late.

4. In formal usage, avoid using *should* in the *that* clause.

5. The following are common adjectives used with *it is* that follow the same pattern as *suggest* and *recommend*.

advisable	good (better, best)	mandatory
crucial	recommend	necessary
desirable	imperative	urgent
essential	important	vital

   It is important that she **call.**

7

Smokers Beware

....

Pronouns
Agreement

"Mind if I smoke?"

▼ FOCUS 1

    A. Meaning   Listen to the story on the tape. What is the main idea? With a partner, write two or three sentences that best summarize the main idea.

    B. Vocabulary   Do you understand the italicized words below? If not, listen to the story on the tape again. Try to understand what the following words mean after hearing them in the story. Can you guess the correct meaning? What words or sentences help you guess? Explain to a partner or your group members what you think these words mean.

controversy	*brain cancer*	*low birth weights*
proposition	*deceptive*	*damaged sperm*
respiratory ailments	*popping up*	*leukemia*

▼ FOCUS 2: Pronouns

    A. The story you have just heard uses many pronouns that students tend to confuse. Read aloud the following sentences. Then try to explain why the boldface pronoun is used.

        Every company has **its** own policy.

        All the companies have **their** own policies.

        Everybody has **his or her** opinion about the policy.

        There is an employee **who** disagrees with the policy.

        The company **that** advertised is being sued.

        The man **whose** wife died of cancer is suing.

        They didn't buy the policy **themselves.**

    B. Edit   Read the sentences below. Look for errors in pronouns. Make the necessary corrections.

    1. Every state has it's own antismoking law.

    2. The politicians which are pushing this laws are worried about there constituents' health.

    C. Listen   Now listen to the story again. Try to list as many pronouns as you hear.

▶ FOCUS 3: Retell the Story

In pairs or as a class, retell the story you have just heard. Your instructor will stop you when you make a mistake. The next student corrects and continues the story.

▶ FOCUS 4: Write the Story

Write a summary of the story in your own words. Be sure to check pronouns and agreement.

Smokers in the United States*

Education (percentage who say they smoke)

Four-year college graduates	13.5%
Some college	23.4%
High school graduates	30 %
Not high school graduates	32 %

If this survey were taken in your country, what do you think the results would be?

American's Views on Tobacco

	Yes	No
Have cigarette manufacturers contribute $1 per carton to charities	59%	24%
Eliminate all cigarette machines so minors can't buy cigarettes so easily	57	25
Eliminate cigarette ads in magazines and newspapers	54	23
Ban smoking in all public places	52	36
Increase the tax on cigarettes to $1 per pack	39	43
Make tobacco products illegal	24	58

*Sources: Centers for Disease Control, Office of Smoking and Health, 1993; "Rebelling against Alcohol, Tobacco Ads," *Wall Street Journal* 14 Nov. 1989.

Compare your views on tobacco to those of Americans from the above survey. Explain your reasoning.

▼ FOCUS 5: Discuss the Story

Discuss the following questions with group members.

1. Do you think companies have a right not to hire a smoker? Give reasons why or why not.

2. If you could vote in the city that wants to prohibit smoking on the street, how would you vote? Explain your answer.

3. If you had been able to vote in California's last election, would you have voted for the twenty-five-cent surcharge on each pack of cigarettes? Give reasons.

4. If you were the judge, how would you decide in the lawsuit against the tobacco companies? Support your opinion.

5. How does the antismoking climate in the United States compare to the situation in your country? Would you like to see any of the antismoking measures in the United States in your country? Explain.

6. Since people in the United States are smoking less, U.S. tobacco companies have increased exports abroad. What do you think of this policy?

▼ FOCUS 6: One-Minute Speech

▼ Choose one of the discussion questions above for your speech.
▼ Outline the points to be made.
▼ Time yourself at home while practicing the speech.

▼ FOCUS 7: Write Your Opinions

▼ Write your opinions on any one of the discussion questions.
▼ Organize your ideas before writing.
▼ Support your opinions with specific examples.

▼ FOCUS 8: Grammar Review

Read the following story. Circle the correct answers. Be prepared to explain your choices.

In (the, 0) United States, a controversy about smoking has been going on since the sixties. New laws (are popping, popped, pop) up all over the country to prohibit people (to smoke, from smoking, to smoking) in enclosed public places. Every (state, states) (have, has) (it's, their, its) own antismoking laws. Even some cities are passing (its, there, their) own laws.

Now in California (there, it, 0) is a city (which, whose, that) mayor wants to make people not (to smoke, smoking, smoke) in the streets. What he proposes is that people (which, who, 0) are addicted to smoking should only be (allowing, allow, allowed) to smoke in the privacy of (one's, their, his/her) own homes. This proposition to prohibit (to smoke, smoking) is the first of (their, it's, its) kind. Voters in this city (would, will) soon decide the fate of smokers.

Not only (smokers are, are smokers) being asked to change (his, one's, their) behavior, (he/she, they) are also being (ask, asked) to pay more for (one's, their, his) habit. During (a, the, 0) last election, Californians (had voted, have voted, voted) to add (a, the, 0) twenty-five- (cent, cents) surcharge on each (pack, packs) of cigarettes. (This, These) extra funds will go to cancer (research, researches).

One new law in Iowa (punish, punishes) minors who (smokes, smoke). If (a, an, the) eighteen year old is (catch, catching, caught) smoking, (he or she, they, one) will (fine, be fine, be fined) a hundred dollars.

These new laws are generating new lawsuits. One famous suit was brought (for, up, against) a tobacco company (**who was, which was,** 0) accused of false advertising. In this case, a woman (**who, which,** 0) dying of lung cancer accused the company officials (to, of) promoting the health benefits of smoking in (**its, it's, their**) advertising when (**they, it**) knew how (are cigarettes dangerous, dangerous are cigarettes, dangerous cigarettes are). The court (would, will) have to decide (whether, weather) or not to punish this company for (**their, its, it's**) deceptive (advertisement, advertising).

Along with a change in laws, there (is, has been, was) a change in attitudes. Some employers don't want smokers (work, worked, working) for (**it, them**). In fact, around 6 percent of companies (do, will, would) not hire a person (**which, who**) smokes. Some companies (even are, are even) firing smokers. One smoker is suing (**his, their**) company for firing him because of his habit. He argues that this firing is (discriminating, discriminatory) because his smoking in private—not on the job—did not hurt his job performance.

As the controversy continues, (**it, there**) is more and more (evidence, evidences) from medical (research, researches) about the dangers of smoking. Studies (**they,** 0) show that more than a thousand people in the United States (**die, dies**) every day from smoking- (relating, related) illnesses. Mothers who (**smoke, smokes**) give birth to children with low birth (weigh, weights) and respiratory ailments. Children of men (**who, which,** 0) smoke are at (more high, higher) risk of brain cancer and leukemia because of the father's (damaging, damaged) sperm. (In addition, However, Thus,) tobacco companies (are insisting, insist) that the medical evidence (**is, are**) unclear. Smokers (**they,** 0) will have to make up (**his or her, their, theirs**) minds by (**theirselves, themself, themselves**). Meanwhile, because cigarette consumption (**has, have**) declined in the United States, American tobacco companies (**they, it, 0**) are exporting (**its, their**) products abroad in hope of increasing consumption.

▼ FOCUS 9: Dictation

From the tape, take a dictation. Check your writing by looking at the transcript in Appendix 2.

▼ FOCUS 10: Storytelling

Now it is your turn to tell members of your group a story. Pay attention to pronouns and agreement.

▼ From a newspaper article, a photograph, or a personal experience, find a story you want to tell.
▼ Introduce new vocabulary to your group.
▼ Limit yourself to two minutes.
▼ Tell the story without reading or memorizing it.
▼ Have your classmates retell the story in pairs.

GRAMMAR REVIEW

Pronouns and Agreement

▼ **Pronouns and Agreement**

1. *Each, every, everybody,* and *everyone* are followed by a **singular noun** and a **singular verb form**. The reference pronoun is singular.

   Every cat has its owner trained.

2. *All* and *some* can be followed by a singular or plural noun depending on whether the noun is countable or uncountable. Note how the reference pronoun **agrees** with the subject.

   Because **all** of their **baggage was** lost, they had to replace **it.**

   Because **all** of their **suitcases were** lost, they had to replace **them.**

3. When possible, change subjects to plural to avoid the awkwardness of *his or her, he or she,* and *him or her.*

   These **children love their** mothers. (Instead of: Every **child loves his or her** mother.)

4. Note that some plural nouns take no *s* in plural form *(people, children, police, teeth, feet),* and some singular nouns end in an *s (economics, news, the United States).*

   Those **people have** themselves to thank.

   The United States has to change **its** trade regulations.

5. *One of the* takes a plural noun and a singular verb.

   One of the students is taking **his** exam early.

6. Note that in the combination *neither . . . nor*, the verb form agrees with the last subject.

> Neither she nor her **children are** here.
>
> Neither her children nor **she is** here.

7. When using *nor* or *or*, a singular pronoun is used.

> If either my mother or sister **wants** to come, **she** can.

8. Avoid confusing *it* with *there*. *It* is used for identification.

> **It's** Emile at the door.

And for adjectives.

> **It's** wrong.

There is used for pronouns.

> **There** is **something** wrong.

And for nouns.

> **There** is **a man** begging.

9. Note the spelling of these reflexive pronouns: themsel*ves*, yoursel*ves*, oursel*ves*, and hi*m*self.

10. When listing a group of subjects, place *I* in the last of the series.

> My sister, my husband, my mother, and **I** ate at home.

Never use *me* as a subject pronoun.

11. After a preposition, an object pronoun must be used.

> **Between you** and **me**, I think the economy is picking up.

12. Avoid confusing *it's* with *its*.

> The cat caught **its** tail in the door. *(Its is a possessive pronoun.)*
>
> When **it's** sunny, they go to the beach. *(It's means "it is.")*

13. A possessive pronoun agrees with the subject, not the object.

He loves **his** mother, and **she** loves **her** father.

14. Use the relative pronoun **who** for people and **which** or **that** for things. **Whom** is an object pronoun for people. See the Grammar Review in Chapter 10 for a more complete review of relative pronouns.

8

Foreign Doctors

·····································

Gerunds

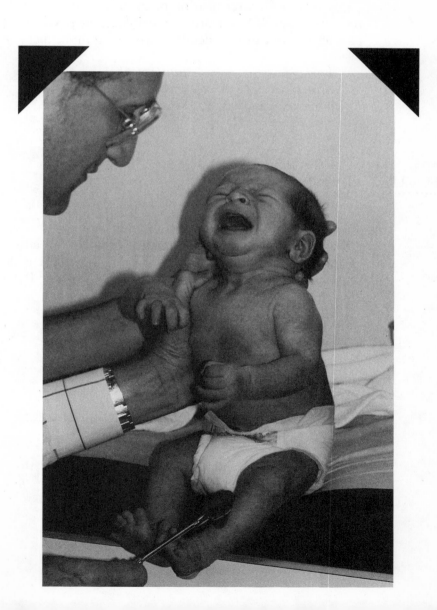

▼ **FOCUS 1**
....

   A. **Meaning**   Listen to the story on the tape. What is the main idea? With a partner, write two or three sentences that best summarize the main idea.

   B. **Vocabulary**   Do you understand the italicized words below? If not, listen to the story on the tape again. Try to understand what the following words mean after hearing them in the story. Can you guess the correct meaning? What words or sentences help you guess? Explain to a partner or your group members what you think these words mean.

   shortage   *tummy ache*
   rural areas   *shrink*
   under the weather

▼ **FOCUS 2: Gerunds**
....

   A. Certain verbs and expressions are only followed by a gerund; others are followed by an infinitive. Some are followed by either a gerund or an infinitive. Do you know which of the following sentences require a gerund, an infinitive, or either? Check the Grammar Review at the end of this chapter when necessary.

   He suggested (to go, going) to this school.

   He advised me (to go, going) to this school.

   I am supposed to (register, registering) in May.

   I look forward to (attend, attending) classes.

   They started (to register, registering) for classes.

   She is busy (to attend, attending) classes.

   What other verbs and expressions do you know that follow the same pattern as the sentences above?

B. **Edit**   Read the sentences below. Look for errors in verb form. Make the necessary corrections.

1. Patients are having difficulty to understand him.

2. She recommended to see another doctor.

C. **Listen**   Now listen to the story again. Try to list as many verbs and expressions followed by the gerund form as you hear.

◤ FOCUS 3: Retell the Story

In pairs or as a class, retell the story you have just heard. Your instructor will stop you when you make a mistake. The next student corrects and continues the story.

◤ FOCUS 4: Write the Story

Write a summary of the story in your own words. Be sure to check the verb forms.

◤ FOCUS 5: Discuss the Story

Discuss the following questions with group members.

1. What are the advantages of the medical system in your country?

2. What are the drawbacks of the medical system in your country? Follow this pattern when answering: The medical system is having *problems (trouble, difficulty) insuring* people. I *recommend (suggest) having* universal coverage for all citizens.

3. Describe a good or bad medical experience that you or someone you know had.

▼ FOCUS 6: One-Minute Speech

- ▼ Choose one of the discussion questions above for your speech.
- ▼ Outline the points to be made.
- ▼ Time yourself at home while practicing the speech.

▼ FOCUS 7: Write Your Opinions

- ▼ Write your opinions on any one of the discussion questions.
- ▼ Organize your ideas before writing.
- ▼ Support your opinions with specific examples.

▼ FOCUS 8: Grammar Review

Read the following story. Circle the correct answers. Be prepared to explain your choices.

In (the, 0) 1970s, because (0, it, there) was (a, the, 0) doctor shortage in the United States, the government decided (**allow, to allow, allowing**) foreign doctors (**work, working, to work**). Still today, rural areas need doctors. So, foreign doctors (have still come, still come, are still coming) to the States to practice. In fact, graduates of foreign medical schools (consist, make out, make up) a fifth of the physicians (practice, practicing) here.

These doctors are (please, pleased) because they receive much (more high, higher) salaries (then, to, than) they did in their (natives, native) countries. Also, being a physician is (consider, considered) a (high, highly) prestigious job. Many foreign doctors, too, are committed to (**serve, serving**) in rural areas (which, where) U.S. doctors are reluctant (**to go, going**). But (there, it, 0) is one big problem—language.

In some hospitals, half (of, of the) doctors are foreign born. Since the staff (come, comes) from (differents, difference, different) countries, not only (patients are having, are patients having, are having patients) difficulty (**understand, to understand, understanding**) the staff, but doctors and nurses (have, are having) problems (**communicate, to communicate, communicating**) with each other. This causes a lot of (trouble, troubles).

A Haitian doctor was (ask, asked, asking) by his patient about (weather, whether) he should see a shrink. The doctor had no idea what (does shrink mean, shrink meant, did shrink mean). Not (to know, knowing, known) that shrink means psychiatrist, he (must, had to, should) ask his patient (to, 0) explain what (was he, he was) talking (about, 0). While the patient explained, the doctor received (a, the) dirty look.

A doctor from Russia had a hard time (**to communicate, communicating**), too. He asked his patient how (was she, she was) feeling. When the patient said, "I'm feeling under the weather," the doctor (was thinking, has thought, thought) that the patient was switching the conversation to the weather. He did not realize that "under the weather" meant that the patient was not feeling (good, well). So the Russian doctor ended up (**to ask, ask, asking**) (to, 0) the patient if it (is, was, were) still raining. His patient looked (confuse, confusing, confused).

A Brazilian doctor spent a long time (**examining, examine**) a six-(years-old, year-old) patient because when the patient complained (to have, about having) a "tummy ache," the doctor had no idea what part of the body "tummy" is. He was (very, too, so) embarrassed to ask. He kept (**to ask, asking**) his patient how long (had his throat, his throat had) been bothering him. Only when the patient pointed to his stomach (did the doctor understand, the doctor understood).

A Chinese doctor had problems (**to examine, examining**) a woman (who, which, 0) was brought into the emergency room. She (told, said) that she felt "like a dog." This meant she felt (terrible, terribly) sick. However, the doctor, (thinking, thought) that she was mentally ill, called (up, 0) a psychiatrist to examine her immediately.

After (**to have, having, have**) such a hard time (**understand, understanding, to understand**) their patients, these doctors are beginning to (**ask, asking**) patients (to, 0) show them where (does it hurt, it hurts) instead of just (**to tell, telling, tell**) them. Pointing will help them (succeed, success, succeeding).

▼ FOCUS 9: Dictation
....

From the tape, take a dictation. Check your writing by looking at the transcript in Appendix 2.

▼ FOCUS 10: Storytelling
....

Now it is your turn to tell members of your group a story with verbs and expressions using gerunds.

▸ From a newspaper article, a photograph, or a personal experience, find a story you want to tell.
▸ Introduce new vocabulary to your group.
▸ Limit yourself to two minutes.
▸ Tell the story without reading or memorizing it.
▸ Have your classmates retell the story in pairs.

GRAMMAR REVIEW

Gerunds

▶ **Gerunds**

1. Some verbs are always followed by a **gerund**.

   > They enjoy swimming.

   These verbs often represent real, fulfilled events. Look at the list below. Try to form sentences with them.

acknowledge	facilitate	quit
admit	fear	recall
anticipate	feel like	recollect
appreciate	finish	recommend
avoid	forget	regret
can't help	get out of	reject
can't stand	give up	relate
consider	imagine	remember
confess	include	report
debate	justify	resent
defer	keep (on)	resume
delay	mention	resist
deny	mind	risk
detest	miss	save
discuss	necessitate	stop
dislike	picture	suggest
dread	postpone	take up
enjoy	practice	tolerate
envision	protest	understand
escape	put off	

2. The verbs *forget, regret, remember,* and *stop* can be followed by a gerund or an infinitive, but there is a change in meaning. Note the differences in the sentences below.

> I **regret to tell** you that I won't be able to come.

> I **regret telling** him what she said about him. (for past)

> He **sometimes forgets to put** on his seat belt.

> He'll never **forget being** in that accident. (for past memories)

> He **stopped buying** the newspaper on his way to work. (*Stop* here means to end an activity. He didn't buy the newspaper anymore.)

> He **stopped to buy** the newspaper on his way to work. (*Stop* here means "stop in order to do something.")

3. *Consider* and *imagine* can also be followed by a gerund or an infinitive depending on meaning.

> I'm **considering quitting** my job. (I'm thinking about it.)

> I **consider her to be** my best friend. (noun phrase + infinitive)

4. *Begin, continue,* and *start* are verbs that can be followed by a gerund or an infinitive with no change in meaning.

> I **started studying** in the afternoon.

> I **started to study** in the afternoon.

5. While most expressions with *to* are followed by an infinitive, the expressions below are followed by a gerund.

> I look forward **to meeting** with you next week.

be accustomed to	be limited to	be resigned to
get used to	object to	revert to
be used to	look forward to	resort to
confess to	be opposed to	be addicted to
be dedicated to	plead guilty to	unaccustomed to
alluded to	according to	adjust to
be confined to	be reconciled to	admitted to
in addition to	be open to	react to

respond to   return to   be committed to
get around to   lead to

6. Below are some common expressions followed by gerunds.

Is that movie **worth seeing?**

be busy   have trouble,
spend time, money   problems,
waste time, money   difficulty
have a good (bad)   be worth
  time   go (swimming,
have fun   shopping, skiing)

7. Note that possessive adjectives are used in front of a gerund.

The teacher suggested **his taking** the course.

In informal spoken English, some say *him*. Note the alternative form of expressing this sentence:

The teacher suggested **that he take** the course.

See the Grammar Review in Chapter 6 for further explanation.

9

Willing to Serve?

....

Modals

Never doubt that a small group of thoughtful, committed citizens can change the world; indeed, it's the only thing that ever has.

— MARGARET MEAD

SOCM (Save Our Cumberland Mountains) is a rural Tennessee citizen's organization working to improve the quality of life in the community. Hundreds of members give thousands of volunteer hours each year to work on issues ranging from the environment to taxes. What do you think of SOCM's motto (Margaret Mead's quote)? Have you seen a community organization which was instrumental in making changes in your country?

▼ FOCUS 1

A. Meaning   Listen to the story of the tape. What is the main idea? With a partner, write two or three sentences that best summarize the main idea.

B. Vocabulary   Do you understand the italicized words below? If not, listen to the story on the tape. Try to understand what the following words mean after hearing them in the story. Can you guess the correct meaning? What words or sentences help you guess? Explain to a partner or your group members what you think these words mean.

do-gooders   *Thirteenth*
nonprofit   *Amendment*
social conscience *outlaws*
                     concede

▼ FOCUS 2: Modals

A. Modals add meaning to a verb. Some differences between modals are very subtle. With a partner look at the list below, and try to group those modals with similar meanings.

must	ought to	would prefer
might	would rather	be able to
should	have to	may
could	had better	can
have got to		

B. Edit   Read the sentences below. Look for errors in modals. Make the necessary corrections.

1. Students must to volunteer; otherwise, they won't graduate.

2. Some should be hesitant about volunteering.

C. Listen   Now listen to the story again. Write down all the modals you hear.

▼ FOCUS 3: Retell the Story

In pairs or as a class, retell the story you have just heard. Your instructor will stop you when you make a mistake. The next student corrects the mistake and continues the story.

▼ FOCUS 4: Write the Story

Write a summary of the story in your own words. Be sure to check the modals when writing.

Views of Citizenship*

Seventy-two percent of one thousand Americans between ages fifteen and twenty-four ranked their life goals as follows:

1. Having a successful career
2. Having a close-knit family life
3. Enjoying life and having a good time
4. Being involved in helping community be a better place

*Source: *Miami Herald* 26 June 1992, based on statistics from a survey taken by the People for the American Way.

1. From what you know of young Americans, how accurate does this survey seem?

2. How do your views compare with those of young Americans?

3. How would the majority of young people in your country rank their life goals? Explain.

▼ FOCUS 5: Discuss the Questions

Discuss the following questions with group members.

1. Have you ever volunteered at a nonprofit organization? Describe your experience.

2. Do public schools have a right to make students do good work? If so, what do you think of the value of such an experience? If not, why not?
3. What do you think of the parents' lawsuit against mandatory volunteering? Would you ever join such a suit? Give reasons why you would or wouldn't join.
4. In New York, a committee has recommended that all lawyers perform at least forty hours of pro bono work (for the public good) every two years. Do you think professionals like lawyers and doctors should be required to do pro bono work?
5. Do you think it is important to give back to the community you live in? Explain.
6. If you were to do volunteer work, what group might you want to work with? Explain.
7. According to a Gallup Poll in 1990, 54 percent of Americans do volunteer work. How do you think this compares to people in your country? Explain your answer.

FOCUS 6: One-Minute Speech

- Choose one of the discussion questions above for your speech.
- Outline the points to be made.
- Time yourself at home while practicing the speech.

FOCUS 7: Write Your Opinions

- Write your opinions on any one of the discussion questions.
- Organize your ideas before writing.
- Support your opinions with specific examples.

FOCUS 8: Grammar Review

Read the following story. Circle the correct answers. Be prepared to explain your choices.

Some high schools across the United States (graduate, are graduating) more and more do-gooders. This is because of a new requirement: you (**will, should, would**) not receive a high school diploma (unless, if) you perform sixty hours of volunteer work. This community service idea was first (propose, proposed, proposing) by the Carnegie Foundation for the Advancement of Teaching, (who, which, 0) felt it was important that students (**must be, were, be**) givers as well as takers.

In (almost, most, most of, most of the) high schools with this requirement, students (**must, ought, have, should**) to volunteer after school, on weekends, and during summer vacations. This service (**must, should, has**) be for a nonprofit organization and (**must, should, has**) benefit the community. Students are (giving, given) a list of organizations to (choose, choice, chose) from. (Despite, Although, However) some students (**may, should, must**) be hesitant when they first start, most get used to (schedule, scheduling) their volunteer work. Many state they look forward to (do, doing) it.

(In addition, However, Thus), quite (a few, few) parents have noticed the positive difference in (his, their) children's behavior after volunteering. One mother talked about how (his, her) son had developed more of (a, the, 0) social conscience about (the, 0) homeless. (However, In fact), many end up working more hours than (require, required). Some work at (soups, soup) kitchens, some at hospitals, and some for environmental groups. Students talk (about, 0) the (possibility, opportunity) to meet people they (**shouldn't, won't, wouldn't, don't**) normally come in contact with.

(Although, However), there are (few, a few) parents (who, which, 0) object to (force, forcing) students to do volunteer work. They feel it is against (the, a, 0) Thirteenth Amendment of the United States Constitution, (0, who, which) outlaws slavery. (While, Since, When) some of these parents concede there is nothing wrong with volunteering, they feel if schools force students to volunteer, students (**will work, work, would work**) unwillingly. (Also, But, So), they say that if students (**must, should, have**) to work, then it is not volunteering. These parents say that (unless, if) the schools drop the requirement, they (**must, should, will**) sue the schools.

(However, Thus, Moreover), most (are agree, agree) that this new requirement (teaches, is teaching) students about serving (his, their) communities. (Despite, In spite of, Although) the opposition, one teacher pointed out that the sixty hours of (requiring, required, require) work just (mean, means) a student (**has, must**) to do fifteen hours a year. He added this (**will, would**) make students (watch, watching, to watch) less television and (be, being, to be) better citizens.

▼ FOCUS 9: Dictation

From the tape, take a dictation. Check your writing by looking at the transcript in Appendix 2.

▼ FOCUS 10: Storytelling

Now it is your turn to tell members of your group a story using modals.

▼ From a newspaper article, a photograph, or a personal experience, find a story you want to tell.

▸ Introduce new vocabulary to your group.
▸ Limit yourself to two minutes.
▸ Tell the story without reading or memorizing it.
▸ Have your classmates retell the story in pairs.

GRAMMAR REVIEW
Modals

▶ **Modals**

1. **Modals** add meaning to a verb. Some of the differences are subtle. Read the examples below to better understand these differences.

Verb	*Indicator of*	*Example*
may	possibility	It may snow tonight.
	permission	May I interrupt you?
might	possibility	It might snow tonight.
	permission	Might I interrupt you? (very formal)
	reported speech	She told me she might go.
should	advisability	He should say he's sorry.
	expectation	She should be here soon.
ought to	advisability	He ought to say he's sorry.
	expectation	She ought to be here soon.
had better	desirability	He had better say he's sorry.
need to	necessity	You need to be at the airport by 1:00 P.M.

Verb	Indicator of	Example
have to	necessity	They have to send their visa application to the embassy.
must	necessity	You must sign your driver's license.
	recommendation	You must come for dinner next week.
	inference	You must be tired after the trip.
be able to	ability	The baby was able to walk before he was a year old.
can	ability	She can play tennis well.
	permission	Can I use your phone?
	possibility	You can improve your accent.
could	past ability	She could play tennis well as a child.
	permission	Could I use your phone?
	possibility	You could improve your accent.

2. The meanings of modals can change in negative form and in past tense. Note the differences in meaning of the following sentences.

   You must tell him. (It is necessary.)

   You mustn't tell him. (It is forbidden.)

   You must have told him. (There is a high probability.)

   She may go. (She has permission or there is a possibility.)

   She may have gone. (There is a possibility.)

3. *Can, could, may, might, will, would, must, had better, would rather,* and *should* are modals followed by the base form of the verb (without *to*).

I'd **rather go** to the movies than to a concert.

We'd **better hurry** up or we'll be late.

Note: Avoid confusing *I'd rather* (*I would rather*, which means "I prefer") with *I'd better* (*I had better*, which means "I should").

4. *Have to, have got to, ought to,* and *be to* are modals followed by the base infinitive (without *to*).

We **have to get** ready for school.

I **ought to be able** to give you a ride.

You **are to tell** me if he insults you.

Ralph Nader

....

Connectors

▶FOCUS 1 ....

A. Meaning   Listen to the story on the tape. What is the main idea? With a partner, write two or three sentences that best summarize the main idea.

B. Vocabulary   Do you understand the italicized words below? If not, listen to the story on the tape. Try to understand what the following words mean after hearing them in the story. Can you guess the correct meaning? What words or sentences help you guess? Explain to a partner or your group members what you think these words mean.

poll	*flip over*	*derogatory*
defect	*uproar*	*promiscuous*
steering wheel	*recall*	*P.I.*

▶ FOCUS 2: Connectors ....

A. This chapter focuses on connectors that often confuse students. Examine the following sentences. Then try to explain the differences in these connectors.

1. **Although** it is raining, they are going to the beach.
   Despite the rain, they are going to the beach.
   In spite of the rain, they are going to the beach.
   It is raining; **however,** they are going to the beach.

2. **During** the concert, he fell asleep.
   While the concert was going on, he fell asleep.
   The musicians were playing. **Meanwhile,** he was sleeping.

Write your own sentences using the boldface words above.

B. Edit   Read the sentences below. Look for errors in connections. Make the necessary corrections.

1. Maybe he was a homosexual. Although, the P.I. turned up nothing in his search.

2. During studying automobile safety, Nader discovered problems.

C. **Listen** Now listen to the story again. Try to list as many words that connect ideas as you can.

FOCUS 3: Retell the Story

In pairs or as a class, retell the story you have just heard. Your instructor will stop you when you make a mistake. The next student corrects and continues the story.

FOCUS 4: Write the Story

Write a summary of the story in your own words. Be sure to check the connectors when writing.

FOCUS 5: Discuss the Story

Discuss the following questions with group members.

1. Is there a consumer movement in your country? If so, what are the people in the movement most concerned with?
2. In what area would you like to see a consumer movement become more active? Give reasons why.
3. What products have you heard of being recalled? Tell the story behind the recall.
4. If you had been the judge, how much would you have awarded to Ralph Nader? Explain why.

FOCUS 6: One-Minute Speech

- Choose one of the discussion questions above for your speech.
- Outline the points to be made.
- Time yourself at home while practicing the speech.

▼ FOCUS 7: Write Your Opinions
....

- ▼ Write your opinions on any one of the discussion questions.
- ▼ Organize your ideas before writing.
- ▼ Support your opinions with specific examples.

▼ FOCUS 8: Grammar Review
....

Read the following story. Circle the correct answers. Be prepared to explain your choices.

In a recent survey, Ralph Nader, a lawyer, came in sixth as the man (**who, which, whom**) people in the United States (**the, 0**) most admire. Who is Ralph Nader? Why (**are, do, have**) so many people look up to him?

He is a man (**whom, who, which**) General Motors wanted to destroy. (**Since, For, After**) graduating from Harvard Law School, Nader (**started, has started**) doing research on the automobile. (**During, While**) studying automobile safety and design, Nader discovered (**0, how**) manufacturers, in (**his, their**) desire for profits, routinely marketed automobiles they knew to be unsafe. Because he felt it was necessary that the government (**regulates, regulate**) the automobile industry(**, or .**) he wrote a book (**which, 0**) called *Unsafe at Any Speed*. In it he described a design problem with the Corvair, a model (**was, which, 0**) manufactured by General Motors. This book exposed how (**was the car dangerous, dangerous the car was**) because (**of, 0**) a defect in the steering wheel. Often when the driver turned a corner, the car (**will flip, would flip, has flipped**) over. There were many (**injure, injured**) people, some of (**them, whom**) died. (**Despite,**

Although) General Motors denied Nader's findings, (**so, but, 0**) the book caused (**a, an, 0**) uproar. In fact, (**after, since, while**) government officials read (**Nader, Nader's**) book, they decided to make General Motors (**recall, recalled, to recall**) its product. It was (**the, 0, a**) first time that the government forced a company (**recall, recalled, to recall**) a product. Also, his book (**rose, raised**) the consciousness of the consumer to understand (**how, 0**) not enough attention was being paid to what causes the deaths and injuries in (**the, 0**) automobile accidents.

The officials at General Motors, (**which, 0**) produced the car, were angry (**about, with**) this decision (**which, 0**) would cost the company (**million, million, millions of**) dollars in repairs and in lawsuits. They decided (**hiring, hire, to hire**) a private investigator to find out something derogatory about Ralph Nader. Maybe he was promiscuous. Maybe he was a homosexual. (**Although, However**), the P.I. turned (**up, out**) nothing in his search. But one day when Nader was on his way home, he (**was finding, found**) a P.I. looking (**in, into, through**) his garbage. In the United States, it is illegal to do that. It is an invasion of (**one, one's**) privacy. Nader had the P.I. (**arrest, to arrest, arrested**) and sued General Motors, for 26 million dollars. Nader, (**who, whom, which**) General Motors wanted to destroy, ended up (**being paid, paying**) almost half a million dollars in an out-of-court settlement. This money went into starting a consumer organization in Washington, DC, (**which, whose**) goal is to protect consumers from being harmed by big corporations (**like, as**) General Motors. Instead of destroying Ralph Nader, G.M. made him a hero.

Today, Nader (**has continued, continues**) fighting for better government and public safety. In fact, years after his first case, Nader is again in (the, 0) court battling General Motors. This time Nader's lawyers claim that General Motors knew for years that its popular pickup trucks were firetraps. (**However, Despite, Although**) this knowledge, General Motors refused to fix the defective fuel tanks. Hundreds of suits against General Motors are still pending.

▼ FOCUS 9: Dictation

From the tape, take a dictation. Check your writing by looking at the transcript in Appendix 2.

▼ FOCUS 10: Storytelling

Now it is your turn to tell members of your group a story using connectors like *although, however, despite, in spite of, during, while,* and *meanwhile.*

▼ From a newspaper article, a photograph, or a personal experience, find a story you want to tell.
▼ Introduce new vocabulary to your group.
▼ Limit yourself to two minutes.
▼ Tell the story without reading or memorizing it.
▼ Have your classmates retell the story in pairs.

GRAMMAR REVIEW

Connectors

◤ Connectors

When connecting ideas, note the different usage and meanings of **connectors**. Those below are most troublesome. Learn how to use them.

1. Some connectors are followed by a noun, while others are followed by a subject and verb.

    In spite of
    Despite } the weather, we went to the beach.

    Although
    Even though
    Despite the fact that
    In spite of the fact that } the weather was bad, we went to the beach.

2. *Because* and *because of* follow a similar pattern.

    Because of the sunny weather, we went to the beach.

    Because it was sunny, we went to the beach.

3. Note how *while* and *during* follow a similar pattern.

    During the lecture, I fell asleep.

    While the teacher gave the lecture, I fell asleep.

4. Now see how some clauses can be shortened.

    Although he was an old man, he sometimes acted like a child.

Although an old man, he sometimes acted like a child.

While I was taking a shower, I sang.

While taking a shower, I sang.

5. The relative pronouns *who, which, whose, whom, where, why, that*, and *when* connect sentences. They introduce clauses that modify a noun or a pronoun.

Ralph Nader wrote a book. It caused an uproar.

Ralph Nader wrote a book **that** caused an uproar.

The relative pronoun *that* replaces the word *it* and comes after the noun it refers to.

6. There are two types of relative clauses: **restrictive** and **nonrestrictive**.

▶ A restrictive clause is essential to the meaning of the sentence. It is never set off by commas and can never be eliminated.

Children who cut classes need counseling.

The relative clause *who cut classes* is essential to the meaning of this sentence, because it describes the particular children who need counseling.

▶ A nonrestrictive clause adds information to the sentence but can be omitted. It is always set off by commas.

Her youngest child, who has been cutting classes, needs counseling.

The relative clause *who has been cutting classes* adds information, but can be omitted.

7. Note the different meanings of relative pronouns.

▶ *who* for people and sometimes animals

The woman who is giving the speech is running for office.

▶ *which* for things and sometimes babies (used in nonrestrictive clauses and less often in restrictive clauses)

My apartment, which is a block from here, is for sale.

▼ *that* for people and things (used in restrictive clauses only and never in nonrestrictive clauses)

The toys that you buy at a discount store are cheaply made.

▼ *whose* for possessive terms for people and less often for things (always followed by a noun)

The woman whose husband you are talking to is from France.

▼ *whom* for object pronouns

The **man to whom** she is talking is her boss.

▼ *where* for places

The **house where** they live is near the beach.

▼ *when* for time

This is the **time when** most people go on vacation.

▼ *why* for reason

This is **the reason why** I chose to study in the United States.

8. Note that *where* is never a subject of a clause and is never used after a preposition. Use *which* or *that* for places when you need a subject or when you have a preposition.

This is the lake **where** he swims.

This is the lake **which** (**that**) he swims **in**.

This is the lake **which** (**that**) is near my house.

9. *That* is an alternative form for both *who, whom,* and *which* except directly after prepositions.

This is the city **in which** I live. (formal)

This is the city **that** I live **in**.

This is the man **to whom** I gave my ticket. (formal)

This is the man **that** I gave my ticket to.

10. Note that *who* is rapidly becoming more acceptable as an alternative for *whom* except when used directly after a preposition. *Whom* is required when it is the object of a preposition.

> This is the man **whom** (**who**) I gave my ticket to.

> This is the man **to whom** I gave my ticket. (*who* is not acceptable here)

To avoid the problem of *who* vs. *whom*, try to drop the relative pronoun when it is the object of its own clause.

> This is the man I gave my ticket to.

11

Finders Keepers

....

Participial Phrases

What Would You Do?

Directions: Interview your partner on how he or she would behave in the following situations. Compare the results of your interview with your classmates'.

1. If I found twenty-five cents in a phone booth, I would . . .

2. If I found a wallet with a hundred dollars, I would . . .

3. If I were accidentally undercharged in a restaurant, I would . . .

4. If the bank mistakenly credited my account with four hundred dollars, I would . . .

5. If the checkout person at a supermarket gave me too much change, I would . . .

▼ FOCUS 1

····································

A. **Meaning** Listen to the story on the tape. What is the main idea? With a partner, write two or three sentences that best summarize the main idea.

B. **Vocabulary** Do you understand the italicized words below? If not, listen to the story on the tape again. Try to understand what the following words mean after hearing them in the story. Can you guess the correct meaning? What words or sentences help you guess? Explain to a partner or your group members what you think these words mean.

armored truck	*sacks*	*constituents*
maple leaves	*screeched to a halt*	*float*
CB radios	*stuffed*	*milling about*
reward		

▼ FOCUS 2: Participial Phrases

····································

A. **Participial Phrases** The story you have just heard uses many participial phrases. These phrases are often used to create a lighter style. To form a participial phrase, the relative pronoun *(who, which, or that)* is omitted and the root verb is changed: the *-ing* form is used for active voice and the *-ed* form of regular verbs is used for passive voice. (Refer to the verb chart on pages 12–14 for the past participle form of irregular verbs.)

The truck, **which was carrying** more than a million dollars, had an accident.
The truck, **carrying** more than a million dollars, had an accident.

The mayor, **who was embarrassed** by the incident, said the thieves were not his constituents.
The mayor, **embarrassed** by the incident, said that the thieves were not his constituents.

Say aloud the following sentences, changing the relative clauses into participial phrases.

1. The lawyer, who is complaining about the settlement, is my friend.

2. The reward that is being given is insufficient.

3. The people who returned the money were honest.

4. Anything that was found should be returned.

5. Anyone who has proof about the police taking the money should report it.

B. Edit   Read the sentences below. Look for errors in participial phrases. Make the necessary corrections.

1. This is the kind of accident makes people believe in miracles.

2. There was a picture of people picked money up from the road.

3. A reward went to anyone was returning the money.

C. Listen   Now listen to the story again. Try to list as many participial phrases as you hear.

◢ FOCUS 3: Retell the Story

In pairs or as a class, retell the story you have just heard. Your instructor will stop you when you make a mistake. The next student corrects and continues the story.

◢ FOCUS 4: Write the Story

Write a summary of the story in your own words. Be sure to use participial phrases.

▼ FOCUS 5: Discuss the Story

Discuss the following questions with group members.

1. If you had been on the highway when the money spilled, what would you have done? Would you have returned the money? Explain why or why not.

2. Do you think people from your country would have behaved differently? Explain how and why.

3. Have you ever found something and kept it? Explain the incident. How do you feel about it today?

4. The expression "The roads are paved with gold" is often said about the United States. Explain what you think this expression means. Do you think it is a true statement today? Do you think it used to be a true statement? Explain why you think so.

5. The expression "Finders keepers, losers weepers" is often said by children in the United States. Explain what you think it means. Do you think that it is an expression people should follow? Describe when people should or should not follow it.

▼ FOCUS 6: One-Minute Speech

▼ Choose one of the discussion questions above for your speech.
▼ Outline the points to be made.
▼ Time yourself at home while practicing the speech.

▼ FOCUS 7: Write Your Opinions

▼ Write your opinions on any of the discussion questions.
▼ Organize your ideas before writing.
▼ Support your opinions with specific examples.

◤ FOCUS 8: Grammar Review

Read the following story. Circle the correct answers. Be prepared to explain your choices.

At 9:30 A.M. (in, on, at) October 28 (in, on, at) Interstate 71 in Ohio, there was (a, an, the) accident, but (a, the, 0) kind of accident (**who, that, 0**) makes people believe (in, on) miracles. The expression "In America the roads are (paving, pave, paved) with gold" seemed to come true.

(A, An, The, 0) armored truck (**carry, carried, carrying**) more than a (millions of, million) dollars was (running, driving) down the interstate. Suddenly, the back door of the truck (has flown, flew, flies) open. The sacks (**held, hold, holding**) the money bounced out and (splitted, split, have split) open. The bills started to float in (the, an, 0) air. Because the truck driver had no idea that he (lost, had lost, has lost) his cargo, he kept on (to drive, driving) to the bank (**which, where**) he was (suppose, supposed) to deliver (the, 0) money. Some of (the, 0) motorists, (**thought, think, thinking**) that the bills were maple (leafs, leaves) because (it, there, 0) was fall, didn't stop (to drive, drive, driving) either. However, when (the, 0) drivers realized that these were not leaves (**which, who, 0**) blowing in the wind, but dollars, they screeched to (a, the, 0) halt. People (**who, which, 0**) had CB radios reported the news. Soon, (the others, others) from a nearby town came to join the crowd (in, on) the highway. (Scooping, Scooped, Scoop) up the money, women, men, and children stuffed (it, them) into (theirs, their) pockets. Some praised the lord for their good fortune. Finally, (0, the, a) police arrived at the scene. Over two hundred people (was, were) milling about. Angry that (a, the, 0) police (came, had come, has come), the crowd accused the officers (to, of) pocketing some of (0, the) dollars (themself, themselves, themselfs). The miracle had come to an end.

The insurance company advertised that (it, they) would give (a, the, 0) 10-percent reward to anyone (**return, returned, returning**) the money. About thirty people returned the money. One telephone repairman (**who, which**) had dreamed (of, to, 0) buying a tractor with the $57,000 he (has, had) scooped up was (the, 0) first to give the money back. He said he (will, would) not have been able to sleep at night if he (would have kept, will have kept, have kept, had kept) the money. Most, however, did not return what they (found, have found, had found). The mayor, (**embarrassing, embarrassed, embarrass**) by the incident (**that, who, 0**) occurred in his town, insisted that those (thiefs, thieves) were not his constituents.

Today the insurance company has one last hope. Someone took (a, the, an, 0) picture of the people (**picked, picking, were picking**) the money up from the road. Insurance officials hope they can identify the thieves from the photo and get (his, their) money back.

▼ FOCUS 9: Dictation

From the tape, take a dictation. Check your writing by looking at the transcript in Appendix 2.

▼ FOCUS 10: Storytelling

Now it is your turn to tell members of your group a story using participial phrases.

▼ From a newspaper article, a photograph, or a personal experience, find a story you want to tell.
▼ Introduce new vocabulary to your group.
▼ Limit yourself to two minutes.
▼ Tell the story without reading or memorizing it.
▼ Have your classmates retell the story in pairs.

GRAMMAR REVIEW
· · · · · · · · · · · · · · · · · · ·
Participial Phrases

▶ Participial Phrases

1. A participial phrase is a verbal phrase with the subject omitted.

    Emile was looking at Evelyn. Emile thought about all she meant to him.

    Looking at Evelyn, Emile thought about all she meant to him.

    Note that the subject of both clauses must be the same.

2. Participial phrases can be in active or passive voice.

    Rachel, **practicing for the play,** forgot to pick up her sister at school.

    Mathew, **invited to talk on Mexico,** gladly accepted.

3. Note that participial phrases can come in front of the subject or right after the subject.

    Swimming in the pool, Laura found the mask she had lost.

    Laura, **swimming in the pool,** found that mask she had lost.

4. Omit the relative pronoun and the auxiliary verb when using a participial phrase after a subject.

    Bruce, **who was taking care of his orchids,** noticed some caterpillars on the flowers.

    Bruce, **taking care of his orchids,** noticed some caterpillars on the flowers.

5. To emphasize the present continuous tense, use *being* with the past participle.

   The book, **now being written,** should be a best-seller.

6. To emphasize the past tense, use *having* (for active voice) and *having been* (for passive voice) with the past participle.

   Having heard about the play, she rushed to buy tickets.

   Having been asked to talk, he started to prepare his speech.

12

The New Illiteracy

······································

If Clauses

FOCUS 1

A. **Meaning** Listen to the story on the tape. What is the main idea? With a partner, write two or three sentences that best summarize the main idea.

B. **Vocabulary** Do you understand the italicized words below? If not, listen to the story on the tape again. Try to understand what the following words mean after hearing them in the story. Can you guess the correct meaning? What words or sentences help you guess? Explain to a partner or your group members what you think these words mean.

flock	*ranked*
cultural illiteracy	*broad spectrum*
reveal	*elite*

FOCUS 2: *If* Clauses

A. Look at the sentences below. Try to explain the differences in meaning in these conditional sentences.

I hope I can go to the movies tonight. If I **am** free, I **will go.**

I can't go to the movies tonight. If I **were** free, I **would go.**

I couldn't go to the movies yesterday. If I **had been free,** I **would have gone.**

Ask your neighbor the following questions, and fill in the blanks with the verbs they use in their responses:

1. Why don't you come to the party tonight? I want to come. If I ____________ my homework, I ____________.

2. Why don't you come to the party tonight? I'm sorry I can't. If I ____________ less homework, I ____________.

3. Why didn't you come to the party last night? Oh gee, I didn't know

about it. If I _____, I _____.

B. Edit   Read the sentences below. Look for errors in the *if* clauses. Make
the necessary corrections.

1. If they would have studied geography, they would had done better.

2. If students spend more time, reading, they would do better.

C. Listen   Now listen to the story again. Try to list as many *if* clauses as
you hear.

▼ FOCUS 3: Retell the Story

In pairs or as a class, retell the story you have just heard. Your instructor
will stop you when you make a mistake. The next student corrects and
continues the story.

▼ FOCUS 4: Write the Story

Write a summary of the story in your own words. Be sure to check the
verb tenses in the *if* clauses.

▼ FOCUS 5: Discuss the Story

Discuss the following questions with group members.

1. From what you know about U.S. education, what impresses you the
most? Be specific.

2. What are the best qualities of the education system in your country?
Give examples.

3. What are some problems in the education system in your country? Describe them.

4. If you could study anywhere in the world, where would you choose? Why?

5. If you were working in the education field, what changes would you like to make?

6. If you had been born in the United States, how do you think your education would have differed?

▌FOCUS 6: One-Minute Speech

▌ Choose one of the discussion questions above for your speech.
▌ Outline the points to be made.
▌ Time yourself at home while practicing the speech.

▌FOCUS 7: Write Your Opinions

▌ Write your opinions on any one of the discussion questions.
▌ Organize your ideas before writing.
▌ Support your opinions with specific examples.

▌FOCUS 8: Grammar Review

Read the following story. Circle the correct answers. Be prepared to explain your choices.

From Taiwan to Algeria and from Japan to Brazil, (thousand, thousands) of foreigners flock to U.S. universities (for, to) study. Those (who, which, 0) come praise the libraries and the research facilities. (The, 0) others praise the informality of the classroom (where, which) teachers encourage students (analyze, to analyze) and question what they read. (Still, Yet, Thus) others praise the atmosphere at universities, which (pushes, push) students (to be, be) creative thinkers as well (than, as, that) critical thinkers. (Still, Yet, Thus), despite the high quality of many universities, tests (given, giving) by the United Nations and by the National Geographic Society (are revealing, reveal) there are some serious problems with (the, 0, an) education quality in U.S. schools. Some call it "cultural (illiterate, illiterates, illiteracy)." This means that (in, on) general-knowledge questions (concern, concerning, concerned) world topics, these students scored very low.

For example, many thought that (the, 0, a) population of the United States was (more, big, bigger) than the population of (the, 0) People's Republic of China. Some said that Jesus Christ (was, is, 0) born in (the, 0) sixteenth century and that Pablo Picasso (was, is, 0) painted in (the, 0) twelfth century. Many (even did not know, did not even know) when Christopher Columbus came to America.

Another area where students scored low was geography. The United States ranked (six, sixth) among ten nations. This survey (is showing, show, showed) that students in Sweden, Germany, Japan, France, and Canada all did better than U.S. students. Britons, Italians, Mexicans, and Russians did (worst, worse). Most disturbing was that 14 percent of the students (testing, tested) in the U.S. schools could not find (his, their) own country (in, on) a map. These students (also had, had also) (little, a little) knowledge about where (was, 0) Vietnam or India (are, is, 0). (Although, Despite, However) U.S. and Russian students were good at locating each other's countries, they lacked geographical knowledge about the rest of the world.

Some blame this cultural illiteracy (for, on) schools. Less than half of (the, 0) students tested in U.S. schools (ever had taken, had taken ever, had ever taken) a course in geography. Critics say if students (**took, would have taken, had taken**) a geography course, they (**would do, would have done, would had done**) better on the test. (The others, Others, Another) say the problem is not the schools but the ethnocentric media, which spend (a little, little) time on international affairs and too (much, many) time on local news. They (also feel, feel also) that if students (**spend, spent, will spend**) less time (to watch, watching) television and more time (to read, reading), they (**would increased, would increase**) their world knowledge. However, there are those (who, 0) feel these comparison tests are worthless because a broad spectrum (of, of the, 0) U.S. population is (been, being, 0) compared with only (the, 0) elite population in other countries. They feel that if only the elite in the U.S. (**was, were, would have been, had been**) tested, they would (**have, had**) surpassed all other countries. Also, if the system (**was, is**) so bad, why do so many come here to study?

Whether these tests are accurate or not, foreign students do complain about how (0, little) their (fellows, fellow) U.S. students seem to know (little, 0) about (others, other) countries.

▼ FOCUS 9: Dictation

From the tape, take a dictation. Check your writing by looking at the transcript in Appendix 2.

▶ FOCUS 10: Storytelling

Now it is your turn to tell members of your group a story using *if* clauses.

▶ From a newspaper article, a photograph, or a personal experience, find a story you want to tell.
▶ Introduce new vocabulary to your group.
▶ Limit yourself to two minutes.
▶ Tell the story without reading or memorizing it.
▶ Have your classmates retell the story in pairs.

GRAMMAR REVIEW

. . . .

If Clauses

▼ *If* Clauses

There are four basic types of conditional *if* clauses.

Real

If the baby **cries,** I **pick** him up.

If the baby **cried,** I **picked** him up.

The words *when* or *whenever* can take the place of *if* in these sentences. Note that the verb tenses are the same in both clauses.

Prediction

If the baby **cries,** I **will give** him a bottle.

Note that the word *will* is not used in the *if* part of the sentence. Yet, the meaning is future.

Unreal Present/Future

If it **were snowing,** he **would go** skiing.

This means it is not snowing, so he will not go skiing. This *if* sentence sets up an unreal condition and speculates about this condition. When talking about the present, in the *if* part of the sentence, note these guidelines:

▼ Use the past tense.
▼ Use *were* not *was.*
▼ Do not use *would.*

Unreal Past

If it **had snowed,** he **would have gone** skiing.

This means that the real situation was that it did not snow, so he did not go skiing. It gives hindsight about this unreal condition. Note these guidelines:

▼ When talking about the past, use the **past perfect** in the *if* part.
▼ Do not use *would* in the *if* part of the sentence.
▼ Note that *would have gone* is the past form of *would go*.
▼ Note that *might have* and *could have* are possible instead of *would have*.

13

Ben and Jerry

....

Inverted Word Order

▶ FOCUS 1

A. Meaning   Listen to the story on the tape. What is the main idea? With a partner, write two or three sentences that best summarize the main idea.

B. Vocabulary   Do you understand the italicized words below? If not, listen to the story on the tape again. Try to understand what the following words mean after hearing them in the story. Can you guess the correct meaning? What words or sentences help you guess? Explain to a partner or your group members what you think the words mean.

plunging	*correspondence*	*biodegradable*
pretax	*course*	*equitable*
harvested	*charities*	*guilty*

▶ FOCUS 2: Inverted Word Order

A. Inversion occurs after certain expressions—usually words that have negative meanings—if the expression comes before the subject. Inversion is used to show more emphasis. Note the difference between the following two sentences.

He **never came** late.

Never did he come late.

The last sentence shows greater strength.

Now practice putting the negative expression at the beginning of the following sentences to make them more emphatic.

1. They hardly ever thought about money.

   Hardly ever _____.

2. She will talk to him under no circumstances.

   Under no circumstances _____.

3. The class does not begin before 6:00.

   Not before 6:00 _____.

4. He not only paid his employees well, but he also gave them long vacations.

   Not only ______________________________.

Now try to make your own sentences with the following words.

Little did she realize
Only once
Not only

B. Edit Read the sentences below. Look for errors in the inverted form. Make the necessary corrections.

1. He didn't go to graduate school, neither his friend.
2. Not only they make a good ice cream, but also do they make a tasty candy.
3. Ben was surprised by the success and so Jerry was.

C. Listen Now listen to the story again. Try to list as many expressions as you hear that are followed by inverted word order.

FOCUS 3: Retell the Story

In pairs or as a class, retell the story you have just heard. Your instructor will stop you when you make a mistake. The next student corrects and continues the story.

FOCUS 4: Write the Story

Write a summary of the story in your own words. Be sure to use the following expressions when writing the story: *nor, not only, more unusual, so.*

▼ FOCUS 5: Discuss the Story

Discuss the following questions with group members.

1. Tell about any business that has tried to help the community in your country or in the United States.

2. Should businesses be forced to give to charities? Explain why or why not.

3. Ben and Jerry are self-made men. Do you know stories of other people who succeeded in business on their own without going to any prestigious schools and without help from their families? Describe their stories. (Try to use some adverbs requiring inverted word order in your description.)

▼ FOCUS 6: One-Minute Speech

▼ Choose one of the discussion questions above for your speech.
▼ Outline the points to be made.
▼ Time yourself at home while practicing the speech.

▼ FOCUS 7: Write Your Opinions

▼ Write your opinions on any one of the discussion questions.
▼ Organize your ideas before writing.
▼ Support your opinions with specific examples.

▼ FOCUS 8: Grammar Review

Read the following story. Circle the correct answers. Be prepared to explain your choices.

Ben and Jerry don't look (like, as) owners of (the, a, 0) multi-million-dollar business. They don't wear suits. Nor (**they have, do they have**) a master's degree (in, on) business. What they look like is two hippies from (the, 0) sixties. Here is their story.

Ben and Jerry (knew, have known, know) each other since they were children. In (the, their, theirs) twenties, they decided (to, 0) open (a, an, the) ice-cream store together. Before (to plunge, plunging) into the business, they decided they (had, have, must) to learn about the ice-cream business. So, they took (a, the, 0) five- (dollar, dollars) correspondence course (in, on) ice-cream making. After that, they opened their first store in Burlington, Vermont, (in, on, at) 1978. At no time (**they realized, did they realize**) that their store (will grow, would grow, grows) into (a, the, 0) 58- (millions, millions of, million) -dollar business. Their ice cream (becomes, became, has become) famous and so (**their business philosophy, their business philosophy did, did their business philosophy**). It is (a, an, 0) unconventional corporation. It pays (its, it's) suppliers more than market prices and pays (its, it's) executive less. It issues a social performance report (analyzes, analyzing) how well (did it do, it did) in the community.

Basically, (Ben's and Jerry's, Ben and Jerry, Ben and Jerry's) philosophy is a business (that, who, 0) makes money in a community (must, have to) give back to the community. So 7.5 percent of (their, its, it's) pretax profits (went, goes, has gone) automatically to charities. More unusual (**is that, that is**) they print (politics, political, politic) messages, (related, relate, relating) to peace and environmental issues, on their ice-cream containers. Also, they believe (on, in) treating their employees (good, well). Pay must be as equitable (as, that, than) possible between top managers and factory workers. Under no circumstances (**anyone can, can anyone**) earn more (then, than, that) five times the salary (earned, earning) by the (most low, lowest) -paid worker.

Ben and Jerry want (to, 0) do more for (the, an, a) environment with a new product—a candy (called, calling, call) Rain Forest Crunch. When you buy this candy, you help save the rain forest because the (brazil, Brazil) nuts (use, used, using) in the candy are (grown, grown up) wild and are (harvesting, harvested, harvest) by the people of the forest. More important (**that is, is that**) 60 percent of the price of the candy (goes, go) to environmental charities.

Not only (**Ben and Jerry are, are Ben and Jerry**) trying to help save the environment, but (**are they also helping, they are also helping**) the needy. The Rain Forest Crunch factory provides job training for people (in, on, at) risk of becoming homeless. And in Harlem, New York, a Ben and Jerry ice-cream parlor (is, is being, 0) built to revitalize the neighborhood and supply jobs for some of (the, 0) homeless (lived, live, living) in a shelter nearby. Ben and Jerry are still working (in, on) making their business (help, helping, to help) the community more. Making (theirs, their) containers biodegradable is their next plan.

▶ FOCUS 9: Dictation
....

From the tape, take a dictation. Check your writing by looking at the transcript in Appendix 2.

▼FOCUS 10: Storytelling

Now it is your turn to tell members of your group a story using negative openings.

▼ From a newspaper article, a photograph, or a personal experience, find a story you want to tell.
▼ Introduce new vocabulary to your group.
▼ Limit yourself to two minutes.
▼ Tell the story without reading or memorizing it.
▼ Have your classmates retell the story in pairs.

GRAMMAR REVIEW

· · · · · · · · · · · · · · · · · ·

Inverted Word Order

▼ **Inverted Word Order**
· ·

The following list presents the cases when **inverted word order** is used.

1. When two ideas are combined, the word *so* is followed by a verb.

    Ben was happy with the product and **so was Jerry.**

2. When two negative ideas are combined, the word *neither* is followed by a verb.

    Ben was not happy with the product and **neither was Jerry.**

3. Both of the sentences below are unreal conditional *if* clauses. Instead of saying *If they were greedy* or *If they had been greedy*, the *if* is dropped, and the word order is inverted. This pattern is used for emphasis and sentence variety.

    Were they greedy, they wouldn't give away so much money.

    Had they been greedy, they wouldn't have given away so much money.

4. When a negative adverb begins a sentence, it is followed by inverted word order. You can say, *He never stole money,* but using the inverted word order strengthens the sentence. It occurs more often in formal writing.

    Never did he steal money.

    The following are other common adverbs used in this way.

rarely	never again	for no reason
never	not until	only once
seldom	at no time	only then
scarcely	not even once	no sooner
barely	on no account	no where
hardly	in no way	more unusual
hardly ever	in few cases	less surprising
not always	not before	
almost never	little	

5. Note the different ways to combine thoughts. Also, note that when the negative word comes before the subject, it is followed by inverted word order.

   Not only did he make money, but he also gave it away.

   He not only made money, but he also gave it away.

   He neither raised salaries nor did he lower them.

   He neither raised nor lowered salaries.

   He did not raise salaries, nor did he lower them.

   He did not raise salaries. Nor did he lower them.

   Neither did he raise salaries, nor did he lower them.

Words and Expressions
That Confuse

"Not ŏ, dummy, o͞o."

▶ Words and Expressions That Confuse

a, an Both words are used for singular countable nouns. *An* is used in front of vowel sounds.

She is working for **an** M.B.A. at **a** university **an** hour from downtown.

advice, advise *Advice* is an uncountable noun for a helpful suggestion. *Advise* is a verb for giving advice.

The teacher **advised** him to listen to his father's **advice**.

Already, all ready *Already* means "coming before in time." *All ready* means "completely prepared."

I've **already** turned in the term paper.
I'm **all ready** for the exam.

also, either, too These words all have the meaning of "and" but word order and usage differ. *Also* appears at the beginning of a sentence, in front of a single verb, in between two verbs, and sometimes at the end of a sentence.

Also, he studies Chinese.
He **also** studies Chinese.
He is **also** studying Chinese.
He is studying Chinese, **also**.

Either appears at the end of a negative sentence.

He doesn't study Chinese, **either**.

When *either* appears at the beginning of a sentence, it has the meaning of "any one of."

"Which newspaper do you want to read?" "**Either** one is fine."

Too often appears at the end of a sentence, but it can also appear immediately after the subject.

He is studying Chinese, **too**.
He, **too**, is studying Chinese.

although, despite, in spite of These words have similar meanings to *but* and are used to join two or more ideas in a sentence. *Although* is a conjunction and often uses two subjects and verbs.

Although it was raining, they went out.

Despite and *in spite of* are prepositions and are followed by nouns or noun clauses.

> Despite the rain, they went out.
> Despite the fact that it was raining, they went out.
> Despite what she said, he went out.

Note that the part of the sentence beginning with *although*, *despite*, and *in spite of* can come at the beginning or end of the sentence depending on emphasis.

> They went out, despite the rain.

> *Note*: The word *of* never follows *despite*. *In spite of* always takes the *of*. The word *but* is never used with these three expressions.
> *Note*: *However* can be used to give a similar meaning of contrast but punctuation differs.

> It rained; however, they went out.
> It rained. However, they went out.

assist, attend *Attend* means "to be or go somewhere," whereas *assist* means "to help."

> He attended class regularly.
> The nurse assisted the doctor during surgery.

arrive in/at *Arrive in* is used for cities and countries.
Arrive at is used for places like airports, stations, and schools.

> He arrived in San Francisco.
> He arrived at the airport.

beside, besides *Beside* means "next to."

> He is sitting beside his wife.

Besides means "in addition to."

> Besides chemistry, she is studying physics.

die, dead, death *Die* is the infinitive and present tense. *Dead* is the adjective form. *Death* is the noun form. *Died* is the past tense and the past participle.

> In 1983, her grandfather died.
> He has been dead for years.

economic, economical Both words are adjectives. *Economical* means "not wasteful." *Economic* refers to the economy.

> Since the government has been having economic problems, Americans have been more economical in their spending.

fall, feel The past tense of *fall* is *fell*. The past tense of *feel* is *felt*.

> He fell in love with her immediately.
> She felt nothing for him.

few, a few   *Few* means "not many." *A few* means "a small but significant number."

She was sad because **few** people called her on her birthday.
She was happy because **a few** people called her on her birthday.

get in/on/out/off   If the subject can stand up, use *get on* and *get off.*

They **got on** the train. They **got off** the bus.

If the subject cannot stand up, use *get in* and *get out.*

They **got in** the taxi. They **got out** of the car.

lay, lie   *Lay* means "to place something down." *Lie* means "to recline" as in bed. Note that the past tense of *lie* is *lay.* The past tense of *lay* is *laid.*

After he **laid** down the newspaper, he **lay** down in bed for an hour.

Note: Lie also means "to make an untrue statement." The verb is regular. The past tense is **lied.**

leave, live   *Leave* means "to part," and *live* means "to exist" or "to reside."

She **leaves** for Tennessee next week.
She **lives** in a small house.

like, as   *Like* is used as a preposition for a comparison. It is followed by a noun.

He really looks **like** his mother.

As is often used as a conjunction to introduce a clause. It is followed by a subject and verb.

Do **as** I told you.

Note: As can also mean "in the role of" or "in the capacity of."

She is working **as** a lawyer.

lose, loose   *Lose* is the infinitive form of a verb. It means "not to find something." *Loose* is an adjective meaning "not tight."

He always **loses** his keys.
The fashionable style is **loose** pants.

make, do   *Make* is often used for constructing or creating something.

The children are **making** a cake.

Here are some phrases commonly used with *make*: a date, a decision, a deal, an excuse, friends, love, a mistake, money, a plan, progress.
    Do is often used for carrying out an activity.

They **do** their homework immediately after school.

Here are some phrases commonly used with *do*: your best, business, cleaning, the dishes, your duty, an exercise, homework, housework, job, research.

murder, murderer   Both words are nouns.

A **murderer** is a person who commits a **murder**.

of, off   The *f* in *of* is pronounced like a *v*. The *ff* in *off* is pronounced like an *f*. *Of* means "belonging to," and *off* is the opposite of *on*.

One **of** the employees turned **off** the light.

principal, principle   *Principal* refers to a head of a school. As an adjective, it means "main" or "chief." *Principle* means "guideline" or "rule."

The **principal** spoke at the graduation ceremony about the importance of having **principles**.

say, tell   *Say* is followed by *to* or *that*. It is used with direct and indirect speech. *Tell* is followed by a direct object or a pronoun. It is often used in indirect speech.

I **said**, "The war is wrong."
I **said that** the war was wrong.
I **said to** him that the war was wrong.
I **told him** that the war was wrong.

quiet, quite   *Quiet* means "soundless" or "calm." *Quite* means "really."

Her parents were **quite** happy about living in the countryside because it was **quiet**.

so, such   *So* is used with adjectives and with *much* and *many*. *Such* is used with nouns.

The demonstration was **so** large.
There were **so** many people demonstrating.
It was **such** a large demonstration.

So . . . that/such . . . that   join sentences.

He is **so** tired **that** he is going to bed.

They arrived at **such** a late hour **that** the party was over.

too, very, so   *Too* has a negative meaning of "too much." Often it is used in the construction "too . . . to." *Very* means "a lot." It is never followed with *to*. *So* means "really."

It's **too** hot **to** study. (I can't study because the heat is too much.)

It's **very** hot, but I'm studying.

It's **so** hot. Can you put on the air conditioner?

turn around/in/over

He **turned around** when he heard a noise behind him.

He **turned in** his homework on time.

Turn the pancake **over** so it can get cooked on the other side.

weather, whether   *Weather* refers to climate conditions. *Whether* means "if."

The **weather** will turn cooler tonight.
I don't know **whether** or not you'll need a blanket.

worse, worst   *Worse* is a comparative adjective; *worst* is a superlative adjective.

This exam was **worse** than the last one.
I received the **worst** grade in the class.

Review Quiz of Words That Confuse

Directions: Read each sentence. If correct, write *C* next to the number. If there is an error in word usage, make the necessary correction.

1. She was enjoying school because when she moved to the dormitory she made few friends right away.
2. Don't worry. You only made a few mistakes on the homework.
3. After going to New York University to get a M.B.A., he decided to work for a American company.
4. He went to work abroad in spite his parents' protests.
5. The school felt that the student deserved a scholarship.
6. The children didn't want their parents to live until they fell asleep.
7. Whatever she tells, you should listen.
8. Why do you think so much people were demonstrating?
9. The students were so fed up with tuition increases and they boycotted classes.
10. The water in the pool is wonderful; it is too warm.
11. The take-home exam had to be turned over before the winter break.
12. Hurricane Andrew was one of the worse natural disasters in Florida.
13. When the students assisted class, they watched less television.
14. When leaving the laundry room, please turn of the lights.
15. We have already studied these words.

16. After going to obedience class, the dog does like he is told.
17. What was the principle reason for the United States to enter World War II?
18. The moment she arrived to Paris, she rushed off to a bakery.
19. After a strenuous workout, the athlete laid down.
20. Since she left him, his creative spirit has been died.
21. The economical problems of his country have been increasing.
22. Will the police catch the murder?
23. Weather he is accepted or not depends on the competition.
24. All the advices he gave helped.
25. When he looses money gambling, he borrows from friends.
26. Watch out for the oncoming traffic when you get off the car.
27. What does she do beside teach?
28. The professor did not smoke and the students didn't, too.
29. Have you made your homework yet?
30. She is making research on cancer.

Answers: 1. a few; 2. C; 3. an M.B.A., an American; 4. in spite of; 5. C; 6. leave; 7. tells you *or* says; 8. many; 9. so fed up with tuition increases that; 10. very warm; 11. turned in; 12. the worst; 13. attended; 14. turn off; 15. C; 16. as he is told; 17. principal; 18. arrived in; 19. lay down; 20. has been dead; 21. economic; 22. murderer; 23. whether; 24. advice; 25. loss; 26. get out of; 27. besides; 28. and the students didn't either *or* and neither did the students; 29. done; 30. doing.

APPENDIX 2

Transcripts of Stories

The Taxi Cab
● ● ● ● ● ● ● ● ● ● ● ● ● ● ● ● ● ●

One rainy day two women decided they wanted to go shopping at Bloomingdale's. They lived on the Upper West Side of Manhattan and were waiting for a bus to take them across Central Park to the store. That day it was raining cats and dogs. The women knew it would be hard to get around the city on such a lousy day. So, when no bus came after a twenty-minute wait, the women decided to try to hail a cab. They tried, but all the cabs were full. Finally, they saw an empty one. They both ran out to the street and waved furiously to make the cab stop. But the empty cab passed them by. They wondered why the cab hadn't stopped for them. Luckily, the light turned red and the cab had to stop. The women ran to the cab, opened the door, and jumped in. The driver turned around and looked surprised. The women didn't understand why. Ignoring his surprised look, they told him to take them to Bloomingdale's.

Off he went. He drove like a madman across Central Park with his foot all the way down on the accelerator. Not only was he swerving in and out of lanes, but he never even bothered to stop at the stop signs. One woman told her friend how scared she was, but she didn't want to be a backseat driver. The other bravely shouted, "Would you mind slowing down?" She also told him that he was driving too dangerously. The driver told the women not to worry as he continued to race to the store. Also, he never put the meter on. The women didn't understand what was going on.

At last, they arrived at Bloomingdale's. Both women felt exhausted. Neither knew how much the trip cost. So, one of the women leaned forward and asked the driver how much they owed him. The driver calmly said, "Nothing, ladies. I just stole the cab."

Women in the United States
•••••••••••••••••••

Since the 1960s, women have been making tremendous strides in the United States. More and more so-called male professions have opened up to female workers. There are now female police officers, firefighters, and construction workers. In the 1980s, the first woman was appointed to the Supreme Court, the first woman became an astronaut, and the first woman ran for vice-president. Medical schools, law schools, and business schools, which used to be predominantly male, are now accepting more and more females. Recently, more women have been graduating from college with a B.A. than men. These new educational choices are leading women into careers with higher salaries. In fact, the number of female lawyers and doctors has substantially increased.

Yet, despite these gains, a double standard still exists between men and women both at home and at work.

At home, although most married women work, 91 percent still do all of the food shopping and cooking. While the number of fathers changing diapers and taking paternity leave is slowly increasing, child-raising falls mainly on women's shoulders. When a child gets sick, usually the mother is the one who stays home. In fact, according to a United Nations Report, most men in the United States do not do housework.

At work, the most visible double standard is unequal pay. Despite the Equal Pay Act, a woman earns about 70 percent of a man's salary for the same job. Recently there have been lawsuits against big corporations like AT&T, General Electric, and Merrill Lynch, which were caught breaking this law and have paid millions of dollars in out-of-court settlements. These successful lawsuits are giving women higher expectations.

Yet, bosses still discriminate against women in hiring and promoting, and husbands still hold back their wives' careers by not doing their share of work at home.

What are women doing now to change these inequalities? They are having fewer children. They are having children later. They are staying in school longer. They are working longer hours. They are speaking against sexual harassment on the job. They are fighting for more affordable child care. They are running for more political offices.

The gender gap is shrinking. But for most women, it is not shrinking fast enough.

Dropouts
•••••••••••••••••••

In West Virginia and in New York, one out of four students drops out of high school. In Washington, DC, the statistics are even worse. One half of all high school students never graduate. Nationwide, the overall dropout rate is 29 percent. Many say they drop out because they are bored. Because of this, U.S. educators are trying to figure out a way to stop this disturbing trend. In Chicago, some schools are throwing pizza parties for potential dropouts. In Milwaukee, some schools are having lotteries for used cars for students who stay in school. In Philadelphia, at-risk students are being awarded after-school jobs and summer jobs for staying in school. But in a New Jersey high school, one principal is using money, not jobs, as an incentive.

This school received a hundred-thousand-dollar grant to pay students who are at risk of dropping out. When these students go to class on time, bring their notebooks, and do their homework, they make five dollars a day. This means students can bring home a twenty-five dollar check every week for attending classes five days in a row. While the program is new, the principal claims that he has already achieved a higher rate of attendance with this money incentive. But some say it is too early to talk about the program's success. Still others feel that even if it does work, using money as an incentive is wrong. There are several programs like this one to keep uninterested students in school.

West Virginian educators, however, have taken a different approach. Instead of paying students, they have decided to revoke a student's driver's license when the student stops going to class. But this ruling is now being challenged by a sixteen-year-old boy. He said that he had to quit going to school because he got his fifteen-year-old girlfriend pregnant. To support his new wife, he said he needed to drive a car. Now the court is deciding what to do in this case. Meanwhile, other states have enacted similar laws. Proponents of these laws say that students cannot understand that dropping out of school means a low-paying job, but they can understand what it means not to be able to drive. However, opponents of this law feel that a school may succeed in getting students to stay in school but it cannot make them learn. If students are not interested in learning, they will not learn.

Wrong Side of the Bed
•••••••••••••••••••

This is a story about an eighteen-year-old foreign student who didn't hear his alarm clock ring so he woke up an hour late for school. Because he was late, he just threw on some clothes and ran out of the house. What a terrible mood he was in! He really felt he had gotten up on the wrong side of the bed.

He ran down the stairs onto the subway platform. While waiting for the train, he picked up a newspaper he saw lying on the bench. After a ten-minute wait, the train arrived at the station. He got onto the crowded train. While the train was speeding down the tracks, he felt a man bumping into him. He thought that the same man had been watching him read his newspaper on the subway platform. All of a sudden, he felt afraid. He remembered how his family had warned him about how dangerous the United States was. He didn't think he was being paranoid. He thought he was being robbed.

Sure enough, when the student put his hand inside his bag, his wallet was gone. Just then the train stopped. He saw the man getting off. The student shouted, "Stop! Thief! He stole my wallet!" Immediately, most of the passengers near the door grabbed onto the man's jacket. Just then the doors of the subway train shut. The man looked shocked as the passengers tore off his sleeve. As the train pulled out of the station, the young man broke down into tears about his lost wallet. Some of the passengers, feeling sorry for the bewildered student, took up a small collection for him so that he could get to school.

When the student arrived home that evening, he was too sad to think. As he walked toward his bed, he felt even sadder. There on the table near his bed, he saw his wallet. He couldn't believe what a terrible mistake he had made. Never again would he leave his house when he was in such a mood. What would he say if he ever saw that man standing at the subway station again?

Drunk Driving
••••••••••••••••••••

The United States has one of the lowest rates of car accidents in the world. Yet, every year about 44,000 people die on the highways in car accidents in the United States. Half of these deaths are caused by drunk drivers. Because of this, stricter laws have been passed recently. California has one of the strictest laws. This law states that if you kill someone while you are driving intoxicated, you will be considered a murderer in the eyes of the law. This is a story about what happened to a thirty-year-old man in California.

One afternoon this man drank four bottles of beer at a bar. After finishing his drinks, he got into his car and drove off. He was speeding. He ran through a stop sign and crashed into another car crossing the intersection. He didn't have enough time to stop. The car that was struck was being driven by a mother; inside were her four children. All of the passengers were killed. However, the drunk driver wasn't injured at all. When the police arrived, they arrested the driver and brought him to court. There he was indicted for murder. After a two-month trial, he was found guilty of murder. He was sentenced to seventy-seven years in prison. While some feel his sentence was justified, others feel he was sentenced too harshly because he had not planned the accident. However, those in favor of the sentence said this was not the first time he had been arrested for drunk driving. Last time he had his driver's license suspended for six months. This time his license has been revoked for life.

The Police Commissioner's Advice
•••••••••••••••••••

A psychologist living in the city was very tired of having his car broken into every month. Typically, someone looking for a radio to steal would smash a window. To have a car window replaced would end up costing a hundred dollars. After having a repairman fix his last window, the psychologist was determined to do something about this vandalism. The repairman recommended that he park his car in a garage and that he never leave it on the street. The psychologist, however, felt a garage would be too expensive. That night, in the newspaper, he read a news item about the police commissioner's advice on car vandalism. It seems that the commissioner had the same problem happen to him. He suggested that car owners leave the doors unlocked so a thief could see that there was nothing to steal. He also recommended that a person not leave anything of value in the car. The police commissioner wrote that since he started this method, he hadn't had his car windows smashed nor had he had his car locks broken. The psychologist thought it was important that he follow the commissioner's advice.

A week after trying this new method, the psychologist had a big surprise. At 8:00 A.M., he went downstairs to leave for work. When he arrived at the car, all the doors were locked. He couldn't understand what was going on. He was so sure that he had left his doors unlocked. Finally, when he unlocked the door, he noticed that the front seat was pulled forward. Also, although he didn't smoke, the car smelled of cigarettes. Suddenly, the psychologist was taken aback when he heard a grunt from the back seat. There was a man in his sixties snoring away. Looking at the homeless man, the psychologist didn't know what to do. Should he let him sleep? Because the psychologist had to go to work, he decided he had to wake him up. The psychologist greeted the homeless man. As he opened his eyes, the homeless man wanted to know what time it was. The psychologist told him that he was on his way to work and he would drop him off somewhere. The homeless man replied that he had nowhere to go so he would get out there. Before leaving, the homeless man suggested that he have someone watch his car so that nobody would steal it. As the old man got out of the car, the psychologist thanked him for his advice.

Smokers Beware
• • • • • • • • • • • • • • • • • •

In the United States, a controversy about smoking has been going on since the sixties. New laws are popping up all over the country to prohibit people from smoking in enclosed public places. Every state has its own antismoking laws. Even some cities are passing their own laws.

Now in California there is a city whose mayor wants to make people not smoke in the streets. What he proposes is that people who are addicted to smoking should only be allowed to smoke in the privacy of their own homes. This proposition to prohibit smoking is the first of its kind. Voters in this city will soon decide the fate of smokers.

Not only are smokers being asked to change their behavior, they are also being asked to pay more for their habit. During the last election, Californians voted to add a twenty-five-cent surcharge on each pack of cigarettes. These extra funds will go to cancer research.

One new law in Iowa punishes minors who smoke. If an eighteen-year-old is caught smoking, he or she will be fined a hundred dollars.

These new laws are generating new lawsuits. One famous suit was brought against a tobacco company accused of false advertising. In this case, a woman dying of lung cancer accused the company officials of promoting the health benefits of smoking in their advertising when they knew how dangerous cigarettes are. The court will have to decide whether or not to punish this company for its deceptive advertising.

Along with a change in laws, there has been a change in attitudes. Some employers don't want smokers working for them. In fact, around 6 percent of companies will not hire a person who smokes. Some companies are even firing smokers. One smoker is suing his company for firing him because of his habit. He argues that this firing is discriminatory because his smoking in private—not on the job—did not hurt his job performance.

As the controversy continues, there is more and more evidence from medical research about the dangers of smoking. Studies show that more than a thousand people in the United States die every day from smoking-related illnesses. Mothers who smoke give birth to children with low birth weights and respiratory ailments. Children of men who smoke are at higher risk of brain cancer and leukemia because of the father's damaged sperm. However, tobacco companies insist that the medical evidence is unclear. Smokers will have to make up their minds by themselves. Meanwhile, because cigarette consumption has declined in the United States, American tobacco companies are exporting their products abroad in hope of increasing consumption.

Foreign Doctors

In the 1970s, because there was a doctor shortage in the United States, the government decided to allow foreign doctors to work. Still today, rural areas need doctors. So, foreign doctors are still coming to the States to practice. In fact, graduates of foreign medical schools make up a fifth of the physicians practicing here.

These doctors are pleased because they receive much higher salaries than they did in their native countries. Also, being a physician is considered a highly prestigious job. Many foreign doctors, too, are committed to serving in rural areas where U.S. doctors are reluctant to go. But there is one big problem—language.

In some hospitals, half of the doctors are foreign born. Since the staff comes from different countries, not only are patients having difficulty understanding the staff, but doctors and nurses are having problems communicating with each other. This causes a lot of trouble.

A Haitian doctor was asked by his patient about whether he should see a shrink. The doctor had no idea what shrink meant. Not knowing that shrink means psychiatrist, he had to ask his patient to explain what he was talking about. While the patient explained, the doctor received a dirty look.

A doctor from Russia had a hard time communicating, too. He asked his patient how she was feeling. When the patient said, "I'm feeling under the weather," the doctor thought that the patient was switching the conversation to the weather. He did not realize that "under the weather" meant that the patient was not feeling well. So the Russian doctor ended up asking the patient if it was still raining. His patient looked confused.

A Brazilian doctor spent a long time examining a six-year-old patient because when the patient complained about having a "tummy ache," the doctor had no idea what part of the body "tummy" is. He was too embarrassed to ask. He kept asking his patient how long his throat had been bothering him. Only when the patient pointed to his stomach did the doctor understand.

A Chinese doctor had problems examining a woman who was brought into the emergency room. She said that she felt "like a dog." This meant she felt terribly sick. However, the doctor, thinking that she was mentally ill, called up a psychiatrist to examine her immediately.

After having such a hard time understanding their patients, these doctors are beginning to ask patients to show them where it hurts instead of just telling them. Pointing will help them succeed.

Willing to Serve?

Some high schools across the United States are graduating more and more do-gooders. This is because of a new requirement: you will not receive a high school diploma unless you perform sixty hours of volunteer work. This community service idea was first proposed by the Carnegie Foundation for the Advancement of Teaching, which felt it was important that students be givers as well as takers.

In most high schools with this requirement, students have to volunteer after school, on weekends, and during summer vacations. This service must be for a nonprofit organization and must benefit the community. Students are given a list of organizations to choose from. Although some students may be hesitant when they first start, most get used to scheduling their volunteer work. Many state they look forward to doing it.

In addition, quite a few parents have noticed the positive difference in their children's behavior after volunteering. One mother talked about how her son had developed more of a social conscience about the homeless. In fact, many end up working more hours than required. Some work at soup kitchens, some at hospitals, and some for environmental groups. Students talk about the opportunity to meet people they wouldn't normally come in contact with.

However, there are a few parents who object to forcing students to do volunteer work. They feel it is against the Thirteenth Amendment of the United States Constitution, which outlaws slavery. While some of these parents concede there is nothing wrong with volunteering, they feel if schools force students to volunteer, students will work unwillingly. Also, they say that if students have to work, then it is not volunteering. These parents say that unless the schools drop the requirement, they will sue the schools.

However, most agree that this new requirement is teaching students about serving their communities. Despite the opposition, one teacher pointed out that the sixty hours of required work just means a student has to do fifteen hours a year. He added this would make students watch less television and be better citizens.

Ralph Nader
●●●●●●●●●●●●●●●●●●●

In a recent survey, Ralph Nader, a lawyer, came in sixth as the man whom people in the United States most admire. Who is Ralph Nader? Why do so many people look up to him?

He is a man whom General Motors wanted to destroy. After graduating from Harvard Law School, Nader started doing research on the automobile. While studying automobile safety and design, Nader discovered how manufacturers, in their desire for profits, routinely marketed automobiles they knew to be unsafe. Because he felt it was necessary that the government regulate the automobile industry, he wrote a book called *Unsafe at any Speed*. In it, he described a design problem with the Corvair, a model manufactured by General Motors. This book exposed how dangerous the car was because of a defect in the steering wheel. Often when the driver turned a corner, the car would flip over. There were many injured people, some of whom died. Although General Motors denied Nader's findings, the book caused an uproar. In fact, after government officials read Nader's book, they decided to make General Motors recall its product. It was the first time that the government forced a company to recall a product. Also, his book raised the consciousness of the consumer to understand how not enough attention was being paid to what causes the deaths and injuries in automobile accidents.

The officials at General Motors, which produced the car, were angry about this decision, which would cost the company millions of dollars in repairs and in lawsuits. They decided to hire a private investigator to find out something derogatory about Ralph Nader. Maybe he was promiscuous. Maybe he was a homosexual. However, the P.I. turned up nothing in his search. But one day when Nader was on his way home, he found a P.I. looking through his garbage. In the United States, it is illegal to do that. It is an invasion of one's privacy. Nader had the P.I. arrested and sued General Motors for 26 million dollars. Nader, whom General Motors wanted to destroy, ended up being paid almost half a million dollars in an out-of-court settlement. This money went into starting a consumer organization in Washington, DC, whose goal is to protect consumers from being harmed by big corporations like General Motors. Instead of destroying Ralph Nader, G.M. made him a hero.

Today, Nader continues fighting for better government and public safety. In fact, years after his first case, Nader is again in court battling General Motors.

This time Nader's lawyers claim that General Motors knew for years that its popular pickup trucks were firetraps. Despite this knowledge, General Motors refused to fix the defective fuel tanks. Hundreds of suits against General Motors are still pending.

Finders Keepers

· · · · · · · · · · · · · · · · · ·

At 9:30 A.M. on October 28 on Interstate 71 in Ohio, there was an accident, but the kind of accident that makes people believe in miracles. The expression "In America the roads are paved with gold" seemed to come true.

An armored truck carrying more than a million dollars was driving down the interstate. Suddenly, the back door of the truck flew open. The sacks holding the money bounced out and split open. The bills started to float in the air. Because the truck driver had no idea that he had lost his cargo, he kept on driving to the bank where he was supposed to deliver the money. Some of the motorists, thinking that the bills were maple leaves because it was fall, didn't stop driving either.

However, when the drivers realized that these were not leaves blowing in the wind, but dollars, they screeched to a halt. People who had CB radios reported the news. Soon, others from a nearby town came to join the crowd on the highway. Scooping up the money, women, men, and children stuffed it into their pockets. Some praised the lord for their good fortune. Finally, the police arrived at the scene. Over two hundred people were milling about. Angry that the police had come, the crowd accused the officers of pocketing some of the dollars themselves. The miracle had come to an end.

The insurance company advertised that it would give a 10-percent reward to anyone returning the money. About thirty people returned the money. One telephone repairman who had dreamed of buying a tractor with the $57,000 he had scooped up was the first to give the money back. He said he would not have been able to sleep at night if he had kept the money. Most, however, did not return what they had found. The mayor, embarrassed by the incident that occurred in his town, insisted that those thieves were not his constituents.

Today the insurance company has one last hope. Someone took a picture of the people picking the money up from the road. Insurance officials hope they can identify the thieves from the photo and get their money back.

The New Illiteracy
....

From Taiwan to Algeria and from Japan to Brazil, thousands of foreigners flock to U.S. universities to study. Those who come praise the libraries and the research facilities. Others praise the informality of the classroom where teachers encourage students to analyze and question what they read. Still others praise the atmosphere at universities, which pushes students to be creative thinkers as well as critical thinkers. Yet, despite the high quality of many universities, tests given by the United Nations and by the National Geographic Society reveal there are some serious problems with the educational quality in U.S. schools. Some call it "cultural illiteracy." This means that on general-knowledge questions concerning world topics, these students scored very low.

For example, many thought that the population of the United States was bigger than the population of the People's Republic of China. Some said that Jesus Christ was born in the sixteenth century and that Pablo Picasso painted in the twelfth century. Many did not even know when Christopher Columbus came to America.

Another area where students scored low was geography. The United States ranked sixth among ten nations. This survey showed that students in Sweden, Germany, Japan, France, and Canada all did better than U.S. students. Britons, Italians, Mexicans, and Russians did worse. Most disturbing was that 14 percent of the students tested in U.S. schools could not find their own country on a map. These students also had little knowledge about where Vietnam or India is. Although U.S. and Russian students were good at locating each other's countries, they lacked geographical knowledge about the rest of the world.

Some blame this cultural illiteracy on schools. Less than half of the students tested in U.S. schools had ever taken a course in geography. Critics say if students had taken a geography course, they would have done better on the test. Others say the problem is not the schools but the ethnocentric media, which spend little time on international affairs and too much time on local news. They also feel that if students spent less time watching television and more time reading, they would increase their world knowledge. However, there are those who feel these comparison tests are worthless because a broad spectrum of the U.S. population is being compared with only the elite population in other countries. They feel that if only the elite in the U.S. had been tested, they would have surpassed all other countries. Also, if the system is so bad, why do so many come here to study?

Whether these tests are accurate or not, foreign students do complain about how little their fellow U.S. students seem to know about other countries.

Ben and Jerry
· · · · · · · · · · · · · · · · ·

Ben and Jerry don't look like owners of a multimillion-dollar business. They don't wear suits. Nor do they have a master's degree in business. What they look like is two hippies from the sixties. Here is their story.

Ben and Jerry have known each other since they were children. In their twenties, they decided to open an ice-cream store together. Before plunging into the business, they decided they had to learn about the ice-cream business. So, they took a five-dollar correspondence course in ice-cream making. After that, they opened their first store in Burlington, Vermont, in 1978. At no time did they realize that their store would grow into a 58-million-dollar business. Their ice cream became famous and so did their business philosophy. It is an unconventional corporation. It pays its suppliers more than market prices and pays its executives less. It issues a social performance report analyzing how well it did in the community.

Basically, Ben and Jerry's philosophy is a business that makes money in a community must give back to the community. So 7.5 percent of its pretax profits goes automatically to charities. More unusual is that they print political messages, related to peace and environmental issues, on their ice-cream containers. Also, they believe in treating their employees well. Pay must be as equitable as possible between top managers and factory workers. Under no circumstances can anyone earn more than five times the salary earned by the lowest-paid worker.

Ben and Jerry want to do more for the environment with a new product—a candy called Rain Forest Crunch. When you buy this candy, you help save the rain forest because the Brazil nuts used in the candy are grown wild and are harvested by the people of the forest. More important is that 60 percent of the price of the candy goes to environmental charities.

Not only are Ben and Jerry trying to help save the environment, but they are also helping the needy. The Rain Forest Crunch factory provides job training for people at risk of becoming homeless. And in Harlem, New York, a Ben and Jerry ice-cream parlor is being built to revitalize the neighborhood and supply jobs for the homeless living in a shelter nearby. Ben and Jerry are still working on making their business help the community more. Making their containers biodegradable is their next plan.

INDEX